TORONTO
SKETCHES 3

971   Filey, Mike, 1941-
.3   Toronto sketches 3 : "the way we were" / Mike
541   Filey. -- Toronto : Dundurn Press, c1994.
Fil   xii, 207 p. : ill.

      Stories originally published in the "The way we were"
      column in the Toronto Sunday Sun.
      07661800   ISBN:155002227X (pbk.)

      1. Toronto (Ont.) - History. I. Title

3603   94NOV29   06/he   1-01036782

TORONTO SKETCHES 3
"The Way We Were"

Mike Filey

DUNDURN PRESS
TORONTO & OXFORD

Editor: Nadine Stoikoff
Printed and bound in Canada by Best Book Manufacturers

The publisher wishes to acknowledge the generous assistance and ongoing support of the **Canada Council**, the **Book Publishing Industry Development Program** of the **Department of Canadian Heritage**, the **Ontario Arts Council**, the **Ontario Publishing Centre** of the **Ministry of Culture, Tourism and Recreation**, and the **Ontario Heritage Foundation**.
        Care has been taken to trace the ownership of copyright material used in the text (including the illustrations). The author and publisher welcome any information enabling them to rectify any ref-erence or credit in subsequent editions.

J. Kirk Howard, Publisher

Canadian Cataloguing in Publication Data

Filey, Mike, 1941–
        Toronto sketches 3

ISBN   1-55002-227-X

1.   Toronto (Ont.) – History.   I. Title.

FC3097.4.F537   1994   971.3'541 C94-932849-9
F1059.5.T6857F537   1994

Dundurn Press Limited	Dundurn Distribution	Dundurn Press Limited
2181 Queen Street East	73 Lime Walk	1823 Maryland Avenue
Suite 301	Headington, Oxford	P.O. Box 1000
Toronto, Canada	England	Niagara Falls, N.Y.
M4E 1E5	0X3 7AD	U.S.A. 14302-1000

For my mother

Contents

Key to Credits:

CNE   Canadian National Exhibition Archives
CTA   City of Toronto Archives
SA   Salvation Army Archives
TH   Toronto Hydro Archives
THC   Toronto Harbour Commission Archives
TTC   Toronto Transit Commission Archives

Photos identified as *Toronto Telegram/Toronto Sun* were acquired by the *Sun* following the *Telegram*'s demise on October 30, 1971.

All uncredited photographs are from the collection of the author.

ACKNOWLEDGEMENTS

I would like to thank the following people and organizations who are always helpful whenever I've contacted them for assistance: Glenda, Patrick, Steve and the rest of the staff at the City of Toronto Archives, Ted Wickson (TTC Archivist), Linda Coban (CNE Archivist), Michael Moir (THC Archivist), Mary-Anne Nicholls (Anglican Church of Canada Archivist), Louise Winton (Commemorative Services of Ontario), staff of the Baldwin Room at the Metro Toronto Public Library, Paul Culliton, Marilyn Bell Di Lascio, Bernie Moser, Bert Wietzes and Cathy Slaney. The people at Dundurn Press, Kirk Howard, Tony Hawke, Jean MacDonald, Nadine Stoikoff and Andy Tong, have always been enthusiastic and supportive.

And a special "thank you" to *Toronto Sun* Chief Librarian Julie Kirsh and her competent staff who make the searching out of "bits and pieces" from the city's past hidden within the microfilm reels of old *Toronto Telegram* newspapers stored in their library fun. And thanks for the cookies, too. In addition, various members of the *Toronto Sun* hierarchy, especially Marilyn Linton, Trudy Egan, John Downing and Paul Godfrey, have always been supportive of my work. Staffers Vena Eaton and Ed Piwowarczyk in the paper's "LIFE" section continue to make my contributions to that section of the paper look good.

It goes without saying (although I better) that without my wife's continued support and encouragement I'd never be able to spend so much time chasing down stories from days gone by. Thanks Yarmila.

INTRODUCTION

Toronto Sketches 3 is, rather obviously, the third time that Dundurn Press has published collections of stories that originally appeared in my "The Way We Were" column in the *Toronto Sunday Sun*. The first two books, *Toronto Sketches* and *More Toronto Sketches* appeared in 1992 and 1993, respectively, and were extremely well received, thereby prompting this third compendium.

Although I did contribute a few pieces to the late, lamented *Telegram* and the daily *Toronto Sun*, unfortunately I can't claim the distinction of having contributed a column to the very first edition of the *Sunday Sun*, the one that rolled off the presses on September 16, 1973. However, it wasn't long before "The Way We Were" became a regular feature, a feature that, according to reader surveys conducted annually, continues as one of the most popular features of the paper.

In the early days, the column wasn't much more than a couple of pictures and a few descriptive words. A few of these early columns have been included in this volume. However, as the column's popularity grew, so, too, did its content, with "The Way We Were" developing into a substantial component of each Sunday's paper.

By my calculations, more than 1,000 "The Way We Were" columns have appeared in the *Sun* over the past eleven or so years.

Please note that the date that the column first appeared is included under the column title. In addition, if the original column requires modification for one reason or another the pertinent comments have been added in italics.

Toronto Sketches 3 contains a little something extra. It includes an explanatory guide to the enormous mural titled *History as Theatre: 200 Toronto Years* that was commissioned by the *Toronto Sun* in honour of the city's bicentennial and created over a period of eighteen months on the Front Street façade of the *Toronto Sun* Building by local artist John Hood. By referring to my guide readers can not only explore two centuries of Toronto history, but more fully appreciate John's extraordinary talents.

TORONTO
SKETCHES 3
"The Way We Were"

SALLY ANN'S 100 YEARS

February 28, 1982

One of the first photos of the Sally Ann Brass Band. *(SA)*

This evening, at 8:00 PM members of the Salvation Army will celebrate a century of service in Canada with a special happening at Yorkminster Park Baptist Church.

The Army will be celebrating the 100 years of caring and helping the needy that have passed since William Freer took to the streets in Toronto in late January 1882.

On July 15, Mayor Thomas Moore, commander of the Salvation Army in the United States, arrived in Toronto to formally establish the Toronto Corps. Over the next few years the members met in Temples on Richmond, Alice and Chestnut streets.

On September 14, 1885, William Gooderham laid the cornerstone of the new "Headquarters" building at the northeast corner of Albert and James streets. The building was opened with great pomp and ceremony in April 1886 by Ballington Booth, son of the Army's founder, General William Booth.

It served for sixty-eight years, being demolished in 1954. The present Salvation Army headquarters building opened, on the same site, in 1956.

In the photo (opposite page) we see the First Canadian Corps Salvation Army Brass Band and it is perhaps the earliest photo of members of the Toronto branch of the Salvation Army in existence. Below: On May 29, 1914, the *Empress of Ireland* was rammed by a Norwegian collier and went to the bottom of the St. Lawrence River in less than fifteen minutes.

Among the 1,012 casualties were 167 members of the Salvation Army, the vast majority being from the City of Toronto. There followed one of the largest funerals in the city's history which was witnessed by 10,000 citizens at Mutual Arena followed by a procession up Yonge Street and a mass burial at Mt. Pleasant Cemetery.

Members of the Army continue to remember the event every May with a service at the gravesite. The white armbands reaffirm "a belief in a life beyond."

The sinking of the ill-fated *Empress of Ireland* resulted in the deaths of 167
Salvation Army members. *(SA)*

BRIDGING THE VALLEY GAP

August 22, 1982

Several weeks ago I was asked to provide some historical details at a plaque unveiling event commemorating the Bloor Street viaduct construction more than sixty years ago. As tomorrow marks the sixty-third anniversary of the opening of this engineering marvel that connects Bloor Street with Danforth, I thought my readers would be interested in my short dissertation given at the unveiling.

"Today we are paying tribute to the wisdom and building creativity of a number of Torontonians who were in various ways responsible for the construction of the Prince Edward Viaduct, known to most modern day citizens as the Bloor Street Viaduct. With the passage of time, the complexity and foresightedness of this engineering marvel tends to lessen. After all, we now have the CN Tower, Eaton Centre and Roy Thompson Hall.

"Surrounding our city in 1910 were other communities, which in 1954 would join Toronto to form Metro Toronto; communities such as Weston, Leaside, Mimico, New Toronto and the Townships of York, Etobicoke, and Scarborough.

"Nestled on the northeastern outskirts of Toronto in 1910 were several small, rather rural neighbourhoods that dawdled along in semi-isolation. Known at various times as Doncaster or Chester and collectively as the Danforth after the sandy main drag that turned to gumbo after a downpour. The area was reachable from the big city only by crossing the Don Valley at Queen Street and heading north on Broadview Avenue, known originally as the road to Don Mills — Don Mills Road.

"On January 1, 1910, the civic election ballot contained a question that asked whether citizens wished a viaduct to be constructed joining Bloor Street to the Danforth. The referendum was soundly defeated by 4,535 votes. The next year, the same question appeared on the ballot. Again it was "no" but by only 567 votes.

"Finally, on January 1, 1913, by a margin of 9,326, the viaduct got the go-ahead.

Let's take a quick look at the total project which will make the evolution of the complete engineering marvel easier to understand.

"The viaduct consists of three integral selections: Bloor, Rosedale and Don. The Bloor or westerly section is essentially a raised viaduct created by filling a ravine with 123,000 cubic yards of sand and stone. This section ran from Sherbourne to Parliament. Next was the Rosedale section which required construction of a 580-foot-long bridge with connecting roadways to Parliament Street and Castle Frank Road. The third (and most ambitious and visible section) was the Don portion. The four main piers of the huge arch are from thirty-five to forty-six feet into bedrock and the longest of the five spans is 281 feet, 6 inches and 125 feet above ground.

"Work on the whole project began on January 17, 1915. The Rosedale section opened October 29, 1917, the Don section, October 18, 1918; and the first streetcars ran across from Bloor to the Danforth on December 15, 1918, saving hundreds of commuters valuable time that had been spent in traffic. Within eight months, the entire 5,267 foot long stretch (just thirteen feet short of a mile) from Sherbourne to Broadview had been macadamized and on August 23, 1919, was opened to vehicular traffic."

The Prince Edward viaduct soon after construction commenced in early 1915.

LEGISLATURE LATER WAS AN INSANE ASYLUM

April 29, 1984

The Front Street Legislative Buildings, c. 1834.

Just west of the new University Square building on the North side of Front Street between Simcoe and John streets, stood, for almost three-quarters of a century, the Legislative Buildings of Upper Canada and later (after 1867) of the Province of Ontario.

Built in 1829, the same year the first Welland Canal opened, these new Legislative Buildings replaced the structure burned during the American invasion of our town in April 1813, and a second government facility built at the foot of Berkeley Street and also destroyed by fire, this time by accident.

In 1841, the provinces of Upper and Lower Canada were united and the government moved elsewhere. The Front Street buildings were turned over to King's College for medical school purposes for a number of years and from 1849 until 1851 they served as an insane asylum.

When the capital of the Province of Canada returned to Toronto in 1856, the buildings returned to their original usage until 1859.

Vacant for a few years, the military used the buildings as a barracks from 1861 until 1867 when with the Confederation of Canada that year, the structures once again served as home for the newly established Ontario Legislature.

In use for the next 25 years, the Front Street buildings were vacated in 1893 when our present Parliament buildings in Queen's Park opened. The old buildings were demolished in 1903.

Another interesting feature of the old Front Street Parliament Buildings has to do with one of its most frequent and distinguished visitors, Oliver Mowat.

Mowat sat in the Provincial Parliament from 1857–64 as member for South Ontario. On October 26, 1872, he became Premier of Ontario and it was while holding this position that he arranged to have the first private telephone line in Toronto connected between his office in the Parliament Buildings and his busy law office on Toronto Street.

The year was 1878 and the company engaged in the telephone business was the Toronto Telephone Despatch Company which was absorbed in 1880 by the newly established Bell Telephone Company.

A FALL STROLL DOWNTOWN

October 3, 1982

The original King Edward Hotel, seen here soon after opening in 1903, has been a downtown landmark for many years.

Autumn is with us, the air is cool, clean and crisp. What better time for a quick walk around downtown Toronto to see if we can find some of the older structures that help make up the rich fabric of history we retain in our city which will celebrate its 150th anniversary just 17 months from now.

Toronto is new; the banks are new, as are most of the hotels and office towers. But tucked away in various places throughout downtown the explorer can still find traces of an earlier Toronto.

Let's go for a short stroll and see if we can find a few of the city's historic gems. Starting at what was the mercantile heart of Toronto, Yonge and King streets, we walk east towards the large spire in the distance. On the south side of King is the newly restored King Edward Hotel. Built in 1903, the King "Eddy," as many Torontonians refer to the hotel, was enlarged in 1922 and today embarks on a new life as one of the city's finest hotels. As we cross Toronto Street, once a lively thoroughfare prior to the opening of Yonge, a little way north on the west side is the handsome Argus building, built in 1853 as the seventh Toronto post office.

Crossing Church Street, so named for the city's first church, is the original Street James' Cathedral. Four churches of the same name preceded this noble structure. Our present St. James' was started in 1850, and the spire, once the tallest on the continent, was completed in 1875.

The next intersection is Jarvis Street, named for Samuel Peters Jarvis who shot one John Rideout in a duel in 1817. On the southwest corner stands the St. Lawrence Hall, built as the city's main social gathering spot in 1850.

Over the years the building faded until demolition was a real threat. Then in the mid-1960s it was felt that restoration of the building would be a fitting project to mark Canada's centennial. The hall was officially reopened, and just in time. The date was December 28, 1967.

A short walk up Jarvis and east on Adelaide is a worthwhile detour that brings us to a minor miracle in the heart of a bustling futuristic city of chrome, aluminum and concrete. On the northeast corner of Adelaide and George Street is the former Bank of Upper Canada, dating back to 1822. A portion of the eastern-most section of the complex is believed to incorporate the walls to Toronto's first post office.

Proceeding south on George, the unique street signs delineate the original streets of Toronto when it was still known as the Town of York. The townsite spreads out to the east.

At George and Front we turn west and on the southwest corner of Front and Jarvis is the St. Lawrence Market housed in a structure incorporating much of the city's first real city hall dating to 1844–45.

West along Front Street we pass the 1892 Gooderham building in the pie-shaped triangle abutting Church Street. Once the head office of the famed Gooderham & Worts distilling company, the building now is a prestige office "tower."

West on Front Street, a walk through Union Station, which is situated between Bay and York streets, on the south side, is a trip calculated to take one back to the days when steam was king. Ready for trains in 1920 massive multi-level government involvement resulted in a lack of tracks into the station for another seven years.

North on Bay we pass the 1937 Toronto Stock Exchange Building soon to move into new high-rise tower. Note the frieze over the front of the building. In particular note the banker's hand in the worker's pocket. Tsk! Tsk!

At the top of the Bay is one of Toronto's best-loved buildings. Opened in 1899 "old" City Hall was the work of local architect Edward James Lennox. It was another building that came close to demolition until a public outcry forced politicians to rethink their motives, and today citizens are as proud of Lennox's masterpiece as they are of Finnish architect Viljo Revell's City Hall of 1965 just across the street.

Walking east on Queen we pass two more landmarks. The exciting Eaton Centre is a newcomer, while across the street Robert Simpsons complex of buildings date from 1895.

As you walk south on Yonge towards King it's hard to believe that the buildings at that particular intersection (one even reaches eighteen storeys into the sky) were the tallest in the country. Today First Canadian Place tickles the sky at seventy-two storeys.

IT DIDN'T USED TO COST A LOT

December 26, 1982

Many people are busy trying to decide what to do this coming New Year's Eve.

Perhaps an evening at a friend's house, skating at City Hall or, what the heck, blow the budget and bring in the New Year with dinner and dancing at the CN Tower or the Royal York.

The old King Eddy and its addition.

Torontonians of a half-century ago had a chance to spend the holidays at the King Edward Hotel where Christmas dinner set you back $2.50. If you had any money left the New Year's Eve Supper Dance had a $15 per person cover charge and included Luigi Romanellis Radio Orchestra for your dining pleasure.

Wednesday, December 22nd
THE DANSANT — Pompeian Ball Room, Parlor Floor from 4.30 to 6 p.m.
A LA CARTE SERVICE ALL DAY— Victoria Room. Special music from 6.30 to 8 p.m.
TABLE D'HOTE DINNER— Pickwick Room $1.50, from 6 to 8.30 p.m.
SUPPER DANCE — Oak Room, 10.30 p.m., until 1 a.m.

Thursday, December 23rd
SPECIAL TEA — Parlor Floor from 4 to 6 p.m.
A LA CARTE SERVICE ALL DAY — Victoria Room. Special music from 6.30 to 8 p.m.
TABLE D'HOTE DINNER — Pickwick Room $1.50, from 6 to 8.30 p.m.
SUPPER DANCE — Oak Room 10.30 p.m. until 1 a.m.

Friday, December 24th
SPECIAL TEA — Parlor, Floor from 4 to 6 p.m.
A LA CARTE SERVICE ALL DAY — Victoria
Room. Special music from 6.30 to 8 p.m.
TABLE D'HOTE DINNER — Pickwick Room
$1.50, from 6 to 8.30 p.m.
SUPPER DANCE — Oak Room, 10.30 p.m. until
1 a.m.

Saturday — Christmas Day
VICTORIA AND OAK DINING ROOM
SPECIAL DINNER from 12 to 2 p.m. — $2.00
CHRISTMAS DINNER from 6 to 9 p.m. with
Special Orchestral Concert — $2.50
CHRISTMAS TEA DANCE — Pompeian Ball
Room, from 4 to 6 p.m. — $1.00
CHRISTMAS SUPPER DANCE — Oak Room
from 9 until midnight, $1.50. Formal

Sunday, December 26th
A LA CARTE SERVICE — Victoria Room 7 a.m.
until midnight
SPECIAL MUSICAL TEA on Parlor Floor
12 Solo Musicians and Assisting Artists.
4.30 until 6 p.m.
DE LUXE DINNER with Orchestral Concert
6.30 to 8 p.m., — $2.00

Thursday, December 30th
SPECIAL TEA — Parlor Floor, from 4 to 6 p.m.
A LA CARTE SERVICE ALL DAY — Victoria
Room. Special music from 6.30 to 8 p.m.
TABLE D'HOTE DINNER — Pickwick Room
$1.50, from 6 to 8.30 p.m.
SUPPER DANCE — Oak Room, 10.30 p.m. until
1 a.m.

Friday, December 31st
New Year's Eve Supper Dance
CRYSTAL BALL ROOM
Dancing to 10.30 p.m.
Luigi Romanelli's King Edward Hotel
Radio Orchestra will Supply the Music
Special Attractions   Favors   Souvenirs
$15.00 per Cover

New Year's Day, 1927
VICTORIA AND OAK DINING ROOM
SPECIAL DINNER, 12 to 2.30 p.m. — $2.00
NEW YEAR'S DINNER, 6 to 9 p.m. — $2.50
with Special Music
SUPPER DANCE — Oak Room. 9 p.m. until
midnight $1.50

BACK TO THE HALLS OF LEARNING

October 10, 1982

Several months ago I wrote about a pictorial history of Weston that had just been published to celebrate the community's centennial. Once again Weston will be the site of an anniversary party. This time it will be at Weston Collegiate Institute. This coming October 15, 16, and 17 the Alumni Association is planning a number of events to which all former W.C.I. students are invited. A "golden tea," an evening dance and buffet dinner and other festivities are planned. Those wishing to participate are asked to contact "WCI 125th" at 416-763-1446.

To help celebrate this milestone, here follows a brief history of the collegiate.

It was through the efforts of William Tyrrell, James Cruickshank and William Nason that the Weston County Grammar School was founded on February 4, 1857. Temporarily housed in the basement of the Methodist Church (now central United) and later transferred to the Weston Library location, the school settled into its new quarters at King and Elm streets in 1858. Public spirited citizens raised the cost of construction, since no government aid was given. After fire destroyed Weston High School in 1875, William Tyrrell, using insurance monies, contracted to erect a new structure which was ready for use the next year.

Weston Collegiate as it was in 1926.

The present school property bordered by William, Pine and MacDonald Avenue was the site of an eight-room school built in 1912. Several additions through the years were added to accommodate increasing enrolment as well as a vocational department. Weston High and Vocational School in 1923 was the first composite school in York County. The familiar W.C.V.S. soon followed. Students travelled from Bolton, Nobleton, Nashville, Woodbridge and Thistletown to attend.

Another new wing in 1953 included a boy's gym, auditorium, library, cafeteria, classrooms and office. Our Centennial Homecoming Celebrations in 1957 were attended by 4,000 former students. A comprehensive history of the school was written by Dora Wattie, entitled *One Hundred Years — A Retrospect* to mark the occasion.

Once again, in the sixties, growing pains necessitated new facilities. While students carried on their studies in the old school, a modern concrete edifice was making its appearance on the football field. June in 1970 saw the last class leave "old" Weston Collegiate to enter the "new" Weston Collegiate Institute in September, 1970. So much had changed! A pool, three-storey auditorium, computer equipment, sound-proof music rooms and many other features were now available. W.C.I. has an enrolment of 1,450 students with teachers and staff of 101 at present.

You've come a long way, W.C.I., from your humble beginnings. Happy 125th Birthday!!

CANADA'S AIRSHIP ERA

October 24, 1982

From the Canadian history lover's best friend in the publishing business, Boston Mills Press, comes a delightful new book on a subject that is almost totally overlooked in this age of supersonic travel, but which half a century ago seemed to be the transportation mode of the future.

I'm referring to the airship which, in turn, is the subject of Barry Countryman's new book, *R100.*

The idea of commercial trans-Atlantic flights utilizing giant airships carrying huge payloads had a real genesis in July 1919, when the R34 made the East Fortune, Scotland-to-Roosevelt Field on Long Island, New York flight in 108 hours, 3 minutes.

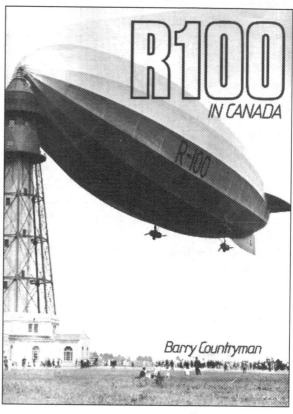

A new Canadian book, *R100*, deals with the era of the commercial airship.

However, the economic situation wasn't right and in 1921 the Secretary of State for Air, Winston Churchill, shelved all the airships initially destined to provide commercial airship flights — the R33, R34, R37, R80 and two German prizes of war, the L64 and L71.

The crash of the R38 which was being built for the U.S. Navy just weeks after Churchill's announcement seemed to be the final nail in the airship casket. However, by 1924, plans had been resurrected by the British government and on May 14 it was announced that two giant airships would be built — one, the R100, by private interests, and the other the R101, by the government itself. It's the former ship that is the subject of Barry's book.

Work started on the R100 in 1924 when Barnes Wallis, designer of the R80, hired N.S. Norway as his chief calculator and engineer. Norway, however, is probably better known for his literary talents as Nevil Shute.

The R100 was 709 feet in length, 133 feet in diameter with fifteen hydrogen gas bags capable of holding 551,890 cubic feet of the highly flammable gas. Up until this time, the airship was primarily developed to serve bases in Egypt, India, Singapore and Australia.

It wasn't until the Imperial Conference of 1926 that Canada got into the act. Having little or no interest in lighter-than-air ships up until that time, Canada's attitude was soon changed when Prime Minister Mackenzie King was convinced by the Secretary of State for Air that for both patriotic and business reasons it was proper and fitting that Canada should construct a mooring mast to enable the country to participate in an ambitious airship demonstration program. Several sites in Canada were surveyed by British experts including the Toronto Jail farm lands north of the city (the buildings stood until very recently at the northeast corner of Yonge Street and Highway #7).

However, after considerable deliberation, it was decided to build the world's most modern airship mast at St. Hubert, seven miles from Montreal. Coincident with the construction of the 205-foot tower, work progressed on the R100 and on December 16, 1929, she made her inaugural flight at Cardington, England. Seven months later, on July 29, 1930, R100 slipped her ring mast and headed westward on her flight to Canada.

Arriving at St. Hubert seventy-eight hours, forty-nine minutes later, the R100 was the major event of the decade (even taking some of the agony out of the Depression).

On August 11, R100 left St. Hubert for a flight over southern Ontario including Niagara Falls, Hamilton and Toronto. Appearing over the Queen City at 4:45 AM and again at 9:18 AM hundreds of thousands marvelled at the giant airship proudly floating overhead. R100 returned to St. Hubert and on August 13, departed Canada for her home base. The "airship era" vaporized less than two months later, when on October 5, R101 was destroyed in a fiery crash in France killing forty-eight on board.

A little over a year later R100 was scrapped. Barry Countryman's book *R100* is a welcome addition to the Canadian aviation library. An added special to this 128-page book is a special 45 rpm record featuring Harold Leonard and the Windsor Hotel Orchestra playing the *R100 Song*.

HYDRO BUILDING HIGHLIGHT

November 7, 1982

A walk along Carlton Street reveals a whole new look to a street that for many years had few major structures in the Yonge to Church Street block.

A recent visit to the Gardens prompted me to look into the history of one of the major structures, the Toronto Hydro head office building.

Toronto Hydro Building going up, 1933. *(TH)*

The first commercial uses of electricity in Toronto occurred in the 1880s when John J. Wright experimented with his electric-powered locomotive at the "Ex" and a small coffee-grinder electric motor in McConkey's Restaurant on Yonge Street. Shortly thereafter, a few electric arc lights were erected on downtown street corners where the brilliant light bathed the intersections in ghostly blue light.

Electricity in those days was generated by burning coal at the main plant of the Toronto Electric Light Company at the foot of Scott Street (just east of today's O'Keefe Centre).

Soon a consortium headed by several city tycoons was ready to send electricity generated by the rushing waters of the great Niagara River spinning giant turbines at the Electrical Development Company plant overlooking the falls.

At 5:28 PM on November 19, 1906, the Davenport Road plant of the Toronto Power Company (as the privately owned enterprise was called) received the first Niagara power to reach the city of Toronto. It became apparent, however, to various government officials that unless steps were taken, private entrepreneurs would have a strange hold on the supply of electricity.

Through the efforts of Adam Beck, the Hydro Electric Power Commission of Ontario (now known as the Ontario Hydro) had been formed a year earlier, and in 1911 Hydro-Electric Commission power generated by Niagara Falls reached the city.

Nine years later the province acquired all the assets of the private electric corporation and hydro had a virtual monopoly on the supply and distribution of hydro-electricity in Ontario.

Coincident with the arrival of "hydro" from Niagara, the City of Toronto established the "Toronto Electric Commissioners" to "manage municipal electric heat, light and power works."

The first three Commissioners were P.W. Ellis (of Ryrie, Birks and Ellis, Jewellers fame), Mayor G.R. Geary and H.L. Drayton. Known better as Toronto Hydro, one of the first projects undertaken by the new operation was to provide street lighting throughout the city using lamp posts every eighty to one hundred feet with one 100-watt bulb on each.

This pattern was the envy of most large cities on the continent.

Referring to the opening paragraph of this article, Toronto Hydro decided in the early 1930s to construct a new head office to replace the badly outdated structure on lower Yonge Street. Land on the north side of Carlton just east of Yonge was acquired in May of 1931. The cornerstone was laid in November 1932, with the handsome structure opening in November 1933, estimated at $1,368,000. The final cost was $1,335,000. Nearby, Maple Leaf Gardens had recently opened (November 21, 1931) as had Eaton's College Street store (October 30, 1930).

Head Office staff in front of new quarters. *(TH)*

METRO'S TOWNS OF YESTERDAY

September 26, 1982

This story is the second half of a two-week series.

This week we continue our trip around Metro and visit some of the communities that today make up our great city:

5. Named "St. Andrews" in 1831 by the first settler in the area, John Grubbe, the community that developed at the intersection of Albion Road and Islington Avenue, soon became known as Thistletown after a prominent local physician, Dr. William Thistle. The name change was necessary as many residents felt mail destined for the small Ontario hamlet would wind up at St. Andrew's in New Brunswick. Thistletown's growth was due in part to the various mills on the nearby Humber River but primarily thanks to the construction of the Albion Plank Road (now Weston Road) that led from the Weston Plank Road (now Weston Road) to Claireville and Brampton giving farmers easy access to and from the markets in the big city of Toronto.

Incidentally, the County Hospital in Thistletown is affiliated with the Hospital for Sick Children and opened in 1928 to take the place of the Hospital's Lakeside Home on Toronto Island which suffered a severe fire in 1915 and was eventually phased out of service.

On June 17, 1933, Thistletown became a Police Village.

6. In 1806 William Cooper, an innkeeper in the Town of York (now Toronto), built a grist and saw mill on the east bank of the Humber River and the settlement that grew around the mill became known as Cooper's Mills. In 1838, that name was changed to Lambton Mills to honour a recent visitor to the community of 500 souls, John George Lambton, first Earl of Durham, Governor-in-Chief of British North America.

North of the mill was the Howland general store run by the Howland brothers, William, Frederick and Peleg. William was a Father of Confederation, Frederick, the Lambton post-master, and Peleg, a vice-president of the Dominion Bank (now T-D) and later president of the Imperial Bank (now CIBC). In 1928 the area changed drastically when the new high-level Dundas Street bridge opened. Today, the Lambton Hotel still stands in the shadow of the bridge, a reminder of the time when Lambton Mills was a prosperous community of the Humber.

7. Todmorden, like Doncaster, Coleman and Little York, were communities that sprang up during the 1850s—1860s period near the Don River/Danforth Avenue area of Toronto. Todmorden in particular was a lively spot developing around a paper mill, brewery and grist mill complex.

The paper mill was the second such enterprise in the entire province. Operated by members of the Helliwell and Eastwood families, it was from the hometown of these robust people, Todmorden near the Lancashire-Yorkshire boundary, that the area derived its name. Mementos of that era can still be seen at Todmorden Mills Park just off Pottery Road in the Don Valley.

8. At Victoria Park Avenue, formerly Davies Road (or simply the Borden Line), and Finch Avenue, a small community called L'Amaroux sprang up in the early 1800s. The name was derived from a pioneering French Huguenot family that moved to New Brunswick following the American Revolution, then to Upper Canada to York County where they settled in Scarborough. The name was spelled in several ways: L'Amoreaux, Lamoraux, L'Amaroux and Lamoureux. Just south of L'Amaroux was O'Sullivan's Corners, named for Patrick O'Sullivan who ran a hotel at the northwest corner of Victoria Park and Sheppard Avenue in 1860.

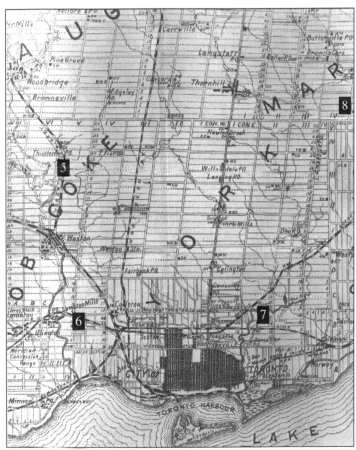

Map shows four of the areas that were incorporated into Metro Toronto:
5. Thistletown, 6. Lambton Mills, 7. Todmorden, 8. L'Amaroux.

ROY THOMSON
STARTED OUT IN A SMALL WAY

October 17, 1982

Toronto's new Roy Thomson Hall has been open for just over a month and the magnificent crystal music box has been received with well-deserved praise from nearly all music lovers.

Even the term Roy Thomson Hall seems to have been accepted by all but the most offended. Actually the subject of this column is Roy Thomson, the man in whose name $4.5 million was donated to assist in the building of the music hall at King and Simcoe streets.

Roy Thomson with one of his early employees, Jack Kent Cooke.
(Courtesy of Toronto Telegram/Toronto Sun)

Thomson was born at 16 Monteith Street in the Church-Wellesley area of our city on June 5, 1894, just nine days before the opening of the new (at that time) Massey Music Hall. This fine structure at Victoria and Shuter streets had been built by Hart Massey in memory of his son Charles Albert who had succumbed in the prime of life to typhoid fever.

Young Roy attended public school until the age of twelve when he was admitted to Jarvis collegiate. He remained at Jarvis just one year, having decided a business college course was more to his liking. Soon he was working at Scythes and Co. In 1812 the family moved to 71 Isabella Street and two years later, when war broke out, Roy was eager to enlist.

Unfortunately, Roy's poor eyesight kept him out of active service, and out of desperation he decided to embark on a new career — farming. But a prairie farmer's life wasn't for Roy and soon he was back in Toronto where he entered the automobile parts business. Another few years and Thomson was in Ottawa still selling sparkplugs and rear axles and still looking for his fortune. Returning to Toronto, Thomson acquired the rights to sell the newest auto part, the De Forest Crosley automobile radio. It soon dawned on Roy there was a fortune to be made in selling these new marvels to car owners in Northern Ontario and in 1929 the whole Thomson family moved to North Bay.

It became apparent that because of poor reception of radio stations located to the south, Thomson could sell more radios if he had his own station in North Bay. So it was that Roy Thomson, having acquired an existing broadcasting licence from Abitibi Company, started station CFCH and he was on his way.

Soon he purchased the *Timmins Press* for $200 down and Thomson never looked back.

Over the years, Roy increased his newspaper holdings to forty-eight in Canada and fifty-eight in the States. In 1953 he moved to Edinburgh, Scotland, where he acquired *The Scotsman* and, in 1957, ITV (Independent Television).

In 1959 he bought the *Sunday Times* and eight years later *The Times*. In 1964, he was created a baron, Lord Thomson of Fleet and of Northbridge in the City of Edinburgh.

The full "Lord Thomson Story" would require pages and pages and I've just skimmed the surface of the life of a great Canadian whose name will be remembered in a truly great Canadian landmark. Lord Thomson of Fleet died on August 4, 1976.

BRIDGING THE GAP

February 13, 1983

On a trip around Toronto Harbour in the fall of last year, I took the photo (centre) as we sailed out of the Western Gap. Dominating the scene is the CN Tower reaching skyward from among the city's skyscraper office buildings. To the extreme right is the Harbour Castle Hilton, and to the right of centre the Toronto Elevators Ltd. structure presently under demolition.

At the base of the tower is the Canada Malting elevator at the foot of Bathurst Street.

The other photo (top), while also shot from the West Gap, was taken in 1911 from the *old* West Gap which was considerably further inland in those days. Landfilling pushed the actual passage further south so that our West Gap is several hundred feet south of the old Gap.

One of the reasons for the change in location was the difficulty many steamship captains had in navigating the gap in rough weather.

Several very serious accidents occurred in this vicinity in the late 1800s. The gentlemen enjoying the outing were guests of the five recently appointed Toronto Harbour Commissioners Messrs. Clarke, Smith, Church, Spence and Gourlay.

View of Toronto from the West Gap, 1911, 1982 and 1994.

The photo is dated December 12, 1911, and there was apparently a relatively mild start to winter that year.

The third photo in the trio above has been added to show the changes in the short period of time since this story first appeared.

ARROW MISSED ITS MARK

February 20, 1983

**The first *Arrow* landing after maiden flight March 25, 1958.
CF-100 chase plane in background.**

Today marks the twenty-fourth anniversary of the death of a remarkable Canadian technological achievement — the Avro *Arrow*.

In 1959 when the *Arrow* project was "put to rest" this magnificent aircraft was in the forefront of development, the state-of-the-art.

Planned as far back as 1949, the CF-105 was to be a supersonic, long-range replacement for the then brand new CF-100; the first Canadian-designed- and built all-weather, twin-engined, two-seater fighter.

In 1953, the Royal Canadian Air Force prepared specification AIR7-3 for a prototype supersonic all-weather fighter. Avro Canada quickly went to work at its Malton plant and soon their initial plans were submitted to and accepted by the RCAF. Design modifications, dimensional refinements and other changes followed.

Sixteen wind tunnel models were built and tested as were several free-flight models and antennae research models. Then on October 4, 1957, the same day as Russia's Sputnik was launched, the first *Arrow* was rolled out of an Avro hanger and introduced to its public. Two months later the *Arrow*'s twin engines were tested, and on March 25, 1958, this incredible aircraft made its first flight. Piloted by Chief Test pilot Jan Zurakowski, RL25201 was airborne for thirty-five minutes accompanied by two chase planes, an F-86 Sabre and a CF-100.

Over the next few months numerous flights were made, several of which were special. For instance, on April 3, 1958, the first level supersonic flight by a Canadian-built aircraft occurred and on April 18 the *Arrow* achieved a speed of Mach 1.96 or almost 1,500 mph, the maximum speed reached during the aircraft testing phase.

During the short life span of the *Arrow*, five aircraft flew a total of sixty-six test flights. All aircraft performed as predicted and while all flights started at Malton, on only one occasion did an *Arrow* venture to another airport. On February 2, 1959, the main Malton Airport runway became inoperative when a TCA Viscount became disabled at the intersection of the two runways available to the *Arrow*.

Quickly plans were made to divert the new jet to Trenton where a safe landing was made much to the surprise of the members of that RCAF base as well as Trentonians who saw the strange aircraft pierce the sky above their town that cold February day.

Optimism ran high at the Avro Canada plant.

There had been some ominous rumblings from Ottawa where John Diefenbaker had recently been returned to power with a landslide victory, March 31, 1958. On September 23 of that year, a press release was issued by the government indicating that the government felt that the days of manned aircraft were numbered and that missiles could and would probably take their place in the 1960s. The *Arrow* and its new jet engine program were to proceed but be re-evaluated in March of 1959.

However, on Friday, February 20, 1959, at 11:00 AM, the Prime Minister rose in the House of Commons and announced that the government had investigated the various military threats against Canada and had concluded that an alternative to the *Arrow* jet aircraft was necessary and, in Dief's words, "the development of the *Arrow* aircraft and Iroquois engine should be terminated now." Continuing he stated, "the government's decisions of last autumn to acquire Bomarc missiles for air defence ... were based on the best expert advice available."

Thus, in one sweeping statement, the *Arrow* and Iroquois projects were ended.

BIG GAS EXPLOSION
LEFT TEN PALS DEAD

March 20, 1983

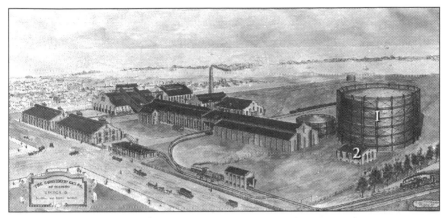

Eastern Avenue was the site of a fatal gas explosion sixty years ago.

Recently, I attended a sober service of remembrance at Birchcliff Heights United Church in Scarborough. The subject of the service was the tragic catastrophe that struck the Consumers' Gas Company February 8, sixty years ago.

A member of Birchcliff Church was one of several heroes that day. Archibald Murdock gave his life as did others in a vain attempt to save his co-workers that cold Thursday in February so many years ago.

Let's look at the circumstances leading up to the event. Consumers' Gas had been established in 1848 and unlike today, the gas that the company supplied to its customers was manufactured gas; that is, it was a by-product of burning coal, oil, anthracite and coke. The coal gas, as it was called, was stored in huge gasometers prior to distribution through mains that snaked all over the city.

In 1923, the year the accident occurred, there were two manufacturing plants in Toronto. Station "A" was at Front and Parliament streets (several gas company buildings still stand: Acme Crane, Toronto Free Theatre, Dalton's) and Station "B" on Eastern Avenue at Booth. In addition, large storage gasometers were located at Station "C" on Bathurst Street opposite Front.

It was at Station "B" that the tragedy occurred. The circumstances were thus:

Gas was being pumped from Station "A" at Parliament Street to the storage tanks at "B" to balance the load," as the operation was called. To reach the gasometer (1) the gas flowed through the valve house (2).

It was in this small building that several employees were removing a flange from a large distribution pipe and, not realizing gas from Station "A" was flowing through the line, removed a large flange and gasket. In flowed the smothering gas quickly overcoming the men. In an effort to aid their friends, others rushed into the building and they themselves were quickly overcome.

By the time it was realized that special precautions had to be taken before entering the gas-filled structure, ten men had been asphyxiated. Ten friends lay on the valve house floor, their lives squeezed out of them by the choking gas.

The victims were John Cotterell, Fred Carey, John Martin, Reuben and Arthur Leadbeater, George Stephen, John Bruce, Frank Rose, Henry Lonsdale and Archibald Murdock.

It was to the memory of these friends that a plaque at Birchcliff Heights was dedicated in that sad, yet proud service held last month.

THE BARCLAY REMEMBERED

April 10, 1983

The Barclay opened as the Hotel Carls-Rite.

Several weeks ago I wrote about the old Barclay Hotel that stood on the northeast corner of Front and Simcoe streets, a site now occupied by a rather nondescript parking lot.

Several readers responded to my request for additional information on the hotel's later days. Let me excerpt from these letters some of their memories of the "Barclay."

Archibald McAulay writes:

"We had organized bowling leagues, beginning at 2 p.m. at a bowling alley on Richmond or Adelaide Street, They only had women pin-setters. If you bowled too fast they would not set up the pins for you.

"If someone in your group was having a birthday, we would arrange to have the party at the Carls-Rite by getting in touch with a nice woman at the hotel.

"She would arrange for a beautiful buffet to be set up in what we call today a rec-room. It was about 40 ft. long and 20 ft. wide in the basement at the hotel. It had a juke box, tables and chairs and lots of room for dancing.

"If it was not a bowling night you could go to the hotel and the night clerk would tell you in which rooms there was a poker game."

"Faithful" reader Sammy Luftspring has these memories:

"My good friends Bill Gold and the late Earl Torno were the proprietors. Hotels and bars in those days were allowed to stay open until 1 a.m., while membership clubs like my Mercury Club had to close at 12 midnight.

"Many nights I would rush over to the Barclay after we closed, to catch the last show. The name of their show room was called the 'Indigo' and it featured some of the great acts of our time, such as Sammy Davis, Billy Daniels and a chorus line of five girls. Joe Louis, the great boxing champion, and my friend, would stay at that hotel when he was in in town. Gary Morton, Lucille Ball's present husband, was a frustrated comic, (I spent some time with him) who was being paid about $250 to $300 a week. He played the room a couple of times a year. I was sorry when the hotel was torn down, but it remains to me some of the happy, nostalgic moments in my life."

Alf Russel has vivid memories of his working days at the hotel:

"I started working at the hotel in 1923 and my first job was in the kitchen. The cooking was done on a coal range about 200 feet long. My wages were $35 a month (because of my age I got $5 less than the other men).

"My meals were included and I started at 7 a.m., had a break in the afternoon and started again at 5 p.m. and worked until 8:30 p.m. I was transferred to the front of the hotel as an elevator operator. This was a better paying job and I got $40 a month, less $2 for the uniform.

"After some time, I became a bell hop, and got $30 a month, less $2 for the uniform but no meals. The difference was to be made up from tips.

"The lobby of the hotel was facing Front Street. There was a revolving door, mostly of brass. The floor was marble tile and the walls walnut wood.

"There was a barber shop with two barbers, a men's room and shoe shine parlor run by Tommy Woo, who also kept all the hotel clocks running.

"Most of the men and women who were playing at the Royal Alex and Princess theatres stayed at the hotel as did all the members of the D'Oyle Carte Opera company. When the Toronto Maple Leaf baseball team played in the International League most of their players stayed at the Barclay. Incidentally, the Leafs were a farm team of the New York Yankees and once a year they came to town to play an exhibition game. All the Yankees stayed at the hotel. Babe Ruth was a guest on one occasion and I was sent to his room to bring his luggage down. It weighed a ton and he didn't even tip me!"

CHASING AFTER OLD WINDMILLS

April 17, 1983

Several weeks ago I received a note from reader Rycke Pothier asking me if I could tell him anything about Toronto's windmill.

He remembered seeing it near the corner of Fleet and Parliament streets.

Actually, the first thing we should discuss is the term Fleet Street. When the new crosstown thoroughfare was laid out by the Harbour Commission on reclaimed land, in the 1920s, the stretch west of the CNE was Lake Shore Boulevard; the midtown section, Fleet Street hooking up in the east with Keating or Commissioner Street. In fact the new Maple Leaf Baseball Stadium at the foot of Bathurst Street was called "Fleet Street flats" for a time after its opening in 1926.

Replica of old distillery windmill at Parliament Street and Lake Shore Boulevard East. It, too, has been demolished.

Fleet Street has since become Lake Shore Boulevard East and West. Therefore, the windmill in Mr. Pothier's letter was at the southeast corner of Parliament and Lake Shore Boulevard East.

This structure was a scale replica of the original windmill that was built in 1832 near the present Trinity and Mill Street intersection. This original structure was put there by Worts & Gooderham (that's how it was named until James Worts died and his son was taken into the business with an appropriate name change) as a means to grind the wheat into flour which was an early

29

product of the G&W partnership.

The windmill was approximately seventy feet in height and required 105,000 bricks, 216 bushels of lime and 100 loads of sand to construct at a total cost of 1,000 pounds ($5,000).

Flour production started on October 5, 1832, and by the end of 1833 nearly 2,500 bushels of flour had been produced at the windmill. Two years later a steam power had replaced the not-always-cooperative winds in providing motive power.

In 1837 or 1839 the roof was blown off the unused mill, and by 1845 the windmill had been demolished. Gooderham & Worts commenced actual distilling operations in 1837 and on November 7 of that year Joseph Lee, a shopkeeper on King Street East became their first customer when he purchased 128 gallons of spirits.

Three years later the distillery's purchases were 22,018 bushels of wheat, 9,650 bushels of barley and 1,632 bushels of rye. Their products were 2,030 barrels of flour and 28,324 gallons of whiskey. The price of the whiskey ranged between thirty cents and seventy-five cents per gallon, depending on the proof.

In 1842 G&W introduced other products — gin, brandy, peppermint and Noyeau, the latter being a sweetened spirit flavoured with butter almonds and peach kernels. The next year saw the purchase of a herd of twenty-two cows, four heifers, several steers and a yoke of oxen to take care of the distilling by-products called slops.

In 1845 the name of the enterprise became the City of Toronto Steam Mills & Distillery. As business increased it became necessary to construct a new distillery which came along in 1861. It was the largest in the country. But that's another story.

Oh, about the replica. It's not known exactly when it was constructed; however, it came down about the time the Gardiner Expressway was being built in the early 1960s.

STATUE HONOURS MARY PICKFORD

May 15, 1983

Born in a nondescript two-storey house at 211 University Avenue, on April 8, 1893, Gladys Marie Smith was the eldest of three children. Her father, John, worked as a purser on the Toronto-Lewiston steamers and one day, while boarding his ship in Toronto, his head struck an unseen overhead pulley.

A blood clot soon formed and within hours the Smith family was fatherless. Shortly thereafter, Dr. G.B. Smith of the Hospital for Sick Children on College Street suggested to Gladys's mother that he and his wife would like to adopt Gladys. The little girl was all set to join the good doctor and his wife who promised her everything.

Mary Pickford's birthplace (centre building), 211 University Avenue, in a photo taken April 28, 1925.

Gladys soon realized the offer did not include her sister and brother, Lottie and Jack. Gladys cried and said "no thanks," she'd remain at home.

A couple of months later, a boarder came to live with the Smiths. Manager of the Cummings Stock Company, the newcomer asked Mrs. Smith whether the girls would like to appear in one of the company's stage productions at the Princess Theatre on King Street (where University Avenue now cuts through). Gladys was five when she appeared on the stage for the first time and she took to it like the proverbial duck to water.

It wasn't long before Gladys appeared regularly in feature presentations. In 1909, the sixteen-year-old (looking twelve) Gladys and her mother met with big-time theatre producer David Belasco. He quickly realized the little girl's potential and after suggested a name change ("How 'bout Mary Pickford?").

Gladys suggested "Mary from Marie and Pickford was my grandmother's maiden name." "Great!" exclaimed Belasco. "And by the way Mary, you'll make your Broadway debut as Betty in *The Warrens of Virginia* on November 11, 1907." And so the legend of "America's Sweetheart" was born.

For the next twenty-three years she reigned as Queen of the silent screen. From her first "one-reeler," *The Lonely Villa* in 1909, Mary captured the heart of theatre-goers in 125 short features and fifty-two full-length films. Her screen farewell was in the 1933 film *Secrets* with Leslie Howard, C. Aubrey Smith and another Canadian, Guelph's own Ned Sparks. Mary always remembered her early life in our city.

In fact she was bothered periodically by a cough which she called her "Eaton cough." When she was a child, Mary's mother would occasionally leave the youngster in her pram while she shopped in Eaton's. Mary developed the croup which became her "Eaton cough."

Mary and her second husband, Douglas Fairbanks, visited Toronto and every time they did, the crowds that turned out to greet the famous Torontonian numbered in the thousands.

Even though she died on May 29, 1979. Mary will soon be coming home again, this time when her sculptured likeness is unveiled in a special public ceremony at 1:00 PM tomorrow.

Thanks to Gino Empry, a Mary Pickford fan, and others; Buddy Rogers, Mary's husband when she died, will unveil the sculpture located on the lawn of the Hospital for Sick Children that was built on the site of Mary's birthplace in 1949–50.

Mary Pickford being interviewed by veteran CFRB newsman Jim Hunter during her hometown visit in 1934.

THE MOVIES WENT "ROUND"
IN CIRCLES

January 15, 1984

In the year 1886, the 120,000 citizens of Toronto had few places of amusement.

Oh yes, there was the Grand Opera House on Adelaide Street West, the Academy of Music hall on King Street West and, of course, Jacob's and Sparrow's place, also on Adelaide.

But it was still quite a lucrative marketplace that William Blackhall, Damascus Mason and George Buchanan found themselves in when they incorporated the Cyclorama Company of Ontario Ltd. and built that strange building on the south side of Front Street West just west of the Walker House Hotel.

The idea was simple enough. The company would display life-size drawings of famous historical events suspended from the ceilings and charge curious customers an admission fee of fifteen cents to be

This unusual round Front Street building once housed cyclorama drawings. It became a machinery company (top), and a rental car outlet (bottom).

escorted around pathways of scaffolding to gaze at the drawings which were illuminated by gas light.

The first historical pageant presented at the Cyclorama was the Battle of Gettysburg and after a two-year stint, this battle was replaced by scenes of the battle of the Sudan.

The final presentation was the Crucifixion following which the panoramic mural idea was replaced by a collection of replicas of the world's most noted paintings under the sponsorship of a new enterprise, the Toronto Art Company.

With the arrival of the magic lantern and illustrated slide lectures the concept lost its uniqueness, and in 1891 the building was gutted and given over to the H.W. Petrie Company as a machinery showroom.

In later years Elgin Ford utilized the building and as a last gasp at remaining useful the old building was turned into a parking garage.

PUTTING TORONTO ON TRACK

April 8, 1984

On October 15, 1851, with 20,000 citizens looking on, Lady Elgin, wife of the Rt. Hon. James, Earl of Elgin and Kincardine, governor-general of British North America and captain-general and governor-in-chief in and over the Province of Canada, Nova Scotia, New Brunswick and the Island of Prince Edward, turned the first sod of the Ontario, Simcoe and Huron Railway.

This ceremony took place in front of the old Parliament Buildings on Front Street, just west of Simcoe Street.

Less than two years later, on May 16, 1853, to be exact, history was made in Toronto when a little steam engine "*TORONTO*" pulling three passenger cars and one freight car left the city to undertake the first scheduled railway trip out of the young city. The destination was Machell's Corners, now Aurora, and the trip was completed, successfully, in a little over two hours.

Within a few weeks the tracks of the O.H. & S. (known affectionately as the Oats, Straw and Hay and soon to be renamed the Northern Railway of Canada) had been pushed through to Bradford, then Allandale (now part of Barrie) and by January of 1855, to Collingwood on Georgian Bay.

Further extensions took the Northern to Orillia, Gravenhurst, Muskoka Wharf and on a spur out of Collingwood, to Meaford.

With the opening of the Northern Railway to Collingwood it became possible to trans-ship grain from the mid-Western United States, that arrived by barge at Collingwood, direct to the 37,000 hungry citizens of Toronto by train thereby eliminating the extra time and money incurred by shipping via Georgian Bay, the Detroit and St. Clair Rivers, Lake Erie, the Welland Canal and Lake Ontario, a trip of at least three weeks even with favourable winds.

In 1888, the Northern became part of the Grand Trunk empire which in turn re-emerged in 1923 as part of the Canadian National Railway System.

The locomotive *Toronto* and her crew pose for the photographer.

TORONTO'S HAD
FOUR BIG UNION STATIONS

April 22, 1984

Not long after the magnificent new Union Station opened in 1873, it became evident that the facility was quickly becoming inadequate to handle the increasing business of both the Grand Trunk Railway and the Canadian Pacific Railway. The latter company had been incorporated in 1881 and was able to gain access to downtown Toronto and the station via the tracks of the Ontario and Quebec Railway, which the company had acquired in 1882.

Alterations to the 1873 station, in the form of trainsheds and an office tower-waiting room facility on Front Street improved the situation, but another thirty-four years had to pass before Toronto could boast that she again had an efficient and modern Union Station.

Construction started on the fourth Union Station to be located on the south side of Front Street, between Bay and York Streets, on Sept 26, 1914.

The three towers of the 1873 Union Station fell to the wrecker's
hammer in 1927.

Construction on Union Station, as we know it today, began in 1914.

Another event had happened just short weeks before, that was to have a major effect on the station project. On August 4, 1914, Britain declared war on Germany and for the next four years Toronto's labour and construction went into defeating "the Hun."

But even as the war dragged on, citizens watched as their new station ever-so-slowly took shape. By 1918, war's end, the exterior walls were complete and in two years both the railway and Post Office Department were able to occupy the offices in the new station. An integral part of the proper operation of the station, and a project that had yet to be addressed, was the grade separation necessary to permit cross-waterfront railway traffic as well as pedestrian and vehicular access via the main north-south traffic arteries.

After many years of negotiating, work on the viaduct began in late 1926 and by October 1927 the project was essentially complete.

Coincident with the viaduct construction, the railway concourse and platform trackage south of the new station was started. Work on both projects had progressed far enough by the summer of 1927 to permit the official, if not public, opening ceremonies to be held during the visit to Toronto by the Prince of Wales and his brother Prince Edward on August 6.

Work continued on the massive viaduct project and finally, on January 31, 1930, with the arrival of CPR train 601 from the east and CN train 28 from the west, Union Station was ready to serve the travelling public.

PIANIST IS HONOURED BY NEW PARK

June 24, 1984

L ast Wednesday, our city gained a new piece of parkland. Though not large, this new piece of greenery called "Sunrise Park" is a welcome addition to the busy Avenue Road-St. Clair Avenue part of Toronto. The little park was dedicated by Mrs. Ernest Seitz And is named "Sunrise" in honour of a song composed by her husband many years ago. Therein lies this week's history lesson.

Ernest Seitz was born in Hamilton in 1892 and at an early age moved to Toronto with his family. He had quite a flair for the piano and while still quite young he went to Berlin to further his musical studies. When

Ernest Seitz co-wrote *The World Is Waiting for the Sunrise* in 1909.

war broke out, Ernest quickly returned home having to forsake a promising concert career. Back in Toronto, he began teaching at the Conservatory of Music. Then while living in apartment 7 at the Bradgate Arms, 465 Avenue Road, he was visited one day by an equally young student-friend from London, Ontario, Eugene Lockhart (Known many years later to movie-goers as Gene Lockhart). Together they took a catchy tune Ernest had created while learning to play the piano as a child, and with Lockhart's lyrics published their new song *The World Is Waiting for the Sunrise* in 1919.

This now world-famous song has been recorded by more than 100 artists including "Duke" Ellington, Benny Goodman, Jack Teagarden, Fritz Kreisler, Ted Lewis and Toronto's own Bert Niosi. In 1951, Les Paul and Mary Ford made Ernie's tune into a million-seller for Capitol Records.

Recently, developer Herman Grad decided to restore the old Bradgate Arms and convert Ernie's former residence into a new luxury retirement hotel in conjunction with the Bradgate project, a nearby house was demolished and a brand new neighbourhood park created. What better name to give to this green space than "Sunrise Park" in tribute to Ernest Seitz, composer of one of the most popular songs ever written in this country and a former tenant of the Bradgate Arms, which itself is now enjoying a new lease on life.

The Bradgate Arms was converted into a luxury hotel.

MEMORIES OF BOWLES LUNCHES

April 28, 1985

One of the most frequently asked questions I get about "old Toronto" has to do with a chain of small restaurants that used to be found downtown. Called Bowles Lunch, they were distinguished by an interior decor that existed almost entirely of white porcelain, everywhere, and the customer would sit in a chair and eat off a small table that formed one arm of that chair. I spoke with Jack Leon who worked for the chain and then for Scott's Restaurants that eventually took over the Bowles locations and he gave me some of the chain's early history.

Bowles was named for one Henry Bowles, a shoemaker from Boston (I wonder if sole was ever on the menu) who travelled considerably and was frequently disappointed by the quality of food he was forced to endure in various eating establishments across the States. He decided to start his own food chain and Bowles Lunch was formed sometime around the turn of the century.

Soon Henry moved north of the border setting up shops in Ottawa, Hamilton, London and Toronto. In fact, by the mid-'50s, there was a total of

Bowles Lunch at the southeast corner of Bay and Queen streets,
September 1923.

five Bowles Lunch outlets in our city. The first two, 7 King Street East and 149 Yonge Street, opened about 1913 with the best remembered 395 Bay Street (at the southeast corner of Queen Street opposite City Hall) opening in 1916. This one was the favourite haunt of more than one mayor of Toronto who'd simply cross the street and have lunch with the ordinary working men. Branches at 173 Bay Street and 11 Bloor Street West followed.

Bowles Lunches were "men only" establishments (by tradition) and had no locks on their doors ... they were open twenty-four hours a day. In the '30s, the restaurants were purchased by Percy Gardiner and Ronald Graham, two prominent Toronto businessmen, and remained in operation until the late '50s when the name was changed to Scott's.

Jack Leon and faithful reader Tom Robinson both remember, with fondness, the special chatter that rang out when orders were placed at Bowles ... "one order of musical fruit" (baked beans), or "a dish of CPR strawberries" (prunes), or "Adam and Eve on a raft" (two poached eggs on toast). Tom also remembers, for those readers who know Montreal, that Cordners Lunch was set up after Mr. Cordner had a chat one day with Henry Bowles and it soon became a popular eating establishment in that city.

Do you have any memories of Bowles?

Bowles Lunch was also on the south side of Bloor Street, west of Yonge, c. 1941.

THE STORY BEHIND
THE MOM'S DAY CHOCOLATES

May 12, 1985

Happy Mother's Day! I wonder how many mothers received chocolates today and of those who did, how many received Laura Secord chocolates? Ever wonder where this truly Canadian product originated? Here's the story.

Frank Patrick O"Connor was born in Deseronto, Ontario, on April 9, 1885. When twelve years of age, Frank moved to Peterboro where he attended a separate school for several years until he'd had enough of that and got a job with the Canadian General Electric Company in that city. Then in 1913, O'Connor left for the big city of Toronto with a recipe for making chocolate candies, a few dollars in his pocket and a dream.

He rented a shop at 354 Yonge Street, just north of Elm Street, converted the upstairs flat into a kitchen and opened Frank O'Connor's Candy Shop. His idea was an instant success and soon the city was studded with candy stores named after the heroine of the War of 1812.

In 1919, Frank decided to go after the sweet teeth south of the border and he opened his first Fanny Farmer Candy Store in Rochester, New York. Realizing Laura Secord, who spied on the Americans during the invasion of Canada in June of

354 Yonge Street, site of O'Connor's first candy store with kitchen upstairs.

1813, was probably not going to be a particularly popular name in the States, he selected the name Fanny Farmer from Fanny Merritt Farmer (1857–1915), a noted culinary expert who wrote the Boston Cooking School Cookbook in 1896.

About 1932, O'Connor acquired approximately 500 acres of property just west of today's Lawrence-Victoria Park intersection and developed a country estate which he called Maryvale after his daughter Mary. Here he bred prize-winning cattle and pure-bred racing horses. It is said that a special road was constructed to allow O'Connor easier access to his estate from his downtown office and factory on lower Bathurst Street and this road later became known as O'Connor Road.

Senator Frank O'Connor (1885–1939)
was the creator of Laura Secord chocolates.

O'Connor also had a summer home at Lake Simcoe where he became good friends with Brother Alexander of the Christian Brothers order who ran the nearby de la Salle camp for boys at Jackson's Point. When O'Connor died, he bequeathed his estate and one-tenth of his fortune to the Brothers. Today, the Christian Brothers administer Senator College School which stands on part of the Maryvale estate adjacent to the original O'Connor home and glass-covered swimming pool.

In addition to being quite a philanthropist, Frank O'Connor was also a highly political animal and was instrumental in the rise to power of both Ontario Premier Mitch Hepburn and Prime Minister Mackenzie King. It was for these latter efforts in Ottawa that O'Connor was elevated to the Canadian Senate in 1935. He died at Maryvale on August 21, 1939.

THE HEYDAY OF HOME DELIVERY

June 2, 1985

I don't know whether you've noticed or not, but another Toronto tradition has vanished. Simpson's home delivery by their familiar dark red, black and cream trucks has been terminated. Now such deliveries are made, under contract, by Canada Cartage.

Actually, I heard about the demise of the Simpson's trucks from a reader, George Kent, of aluminum siding fame. He invited me to meet his eighty-five-year-young father, Gilbert, who had been a Simpson's driver for some forty-seven years prior to his retirement back in 1964. If anyone could relive the heyday of the home delivery it was Gilbert.

AMAZING MEMORY

I visited Mr. and Mrs. Kent at their Leaside home one evening several weeks ago and for two hours I was fascinated by Mr. Kent's fabulous ability to recall things he did or saw more than sixty years ago.

Born in 1899, at 122 Dundas Street East (in those days it was 86 Wilton Avenue) at the corner of Dalhousie, Gil (if I may be so bold as to use his nickname) went to the old public school at the top of Victoria Street. As a boy he had several delivery jobs where he would meet old-time Toronto businessmen like Jesse Applegath, the haberdasher, and Frank O'Connor who, as I wrote a few weeks ago, was the founder of Laura Secord chocolates. Gil surprised me when he mentioned picking up an order at Frank O'Connor's candy store at 354 Yonge Street. He even remembered the address sixty years later!

After several of these delivery jobs, where he split the five-cent delivery charge with the boss, he went to work for the Robert Simpson Company in 1917. In those far-off days, long before automotive power took over, wagons (sleighs in the winter) pulled by horses were the rule. Gil remembers his first steed, "Joe," who was one of the 275 horses, usually dapple-grey in color (Eaton's had the chestnuts), that pulled the always clean Simpson's wagons around town. Gil's route took him through the streets of east-central Toronto. Later, he moved into the "wilds" of north Toronto.

Amazing as it may sound today the drivers made three deliveries daily, six days a week, travelling back to the Mutual Street depot each time to reload the delivery wagon. In fact, at Christmas time, when the deliveries just had to get there, department store drivers could be seen making deliveries as late as 2:30 in the morning! All this for, in Gil's case, twenty-four dollars a week.

Gilbert Kent and Joe make deliveries in Leaside in the winter of 1923.
(Courtesy George Kent)

When drivers reached the age of fifty, the insurance company made them give up the small parcel delivery job and move to the delivery of heavy furniture and appliances. It was believed that the running associated with the delivery of small packages (jogging's nothing new to Gil) was harder on the heart than lifting heavy objects.

MOVED TO TRUCKS

When the horses were retired, many to logging camps in northern Ontario, in the late '20s, Gil moved onto trucks, but when the war broke out in 1939 and gas and rubber rationing went into effect, nearby farms were scoured and a large number of horses found themselves back on the streets of Toronto.

Mr. Kent stayed with the Simpson organization for nearly half a century until his retirement in 1964. Not used to staying home, Gil found some less-demanding work and didn't fully retire for another few years. Today, Mr. and Mrs. Kent remember an earlier Toronto with obvious fondness. Best wishes Mr. Kent, and thanks for the memories.

THE ARCH THAT WENT TO THE EX

August 25, 1985

We're well into the 107th edition of the CNE.

Over the years, there have been all sorts of attractions at the Ex, from the newest automobiles and transit vehicles to the latest in agricultural implements and hi-fi's.

One of the strangest things to find its way to the fair was the huge arch built by the Independent Order of Foresters in 1901. It originally stood in the intersection of Bay and Richmond streets, downtown. This huge structure was moved to the site of the 1902 Exhibition, where it remained for years, before it deteriorated and was destroyed.

The IOF, creators of this magnificent piece of turn-of-the-century art work, had their offices in the Temple Building which stood at the northwest corner of Bay and Adelaide streets.

In 1901, it was announced that the Duke and Duchess of Cornwall and York (who were to become King George V and his queen, Mary) were to visit Toronto. The IOF, a cooperative insurance society, decided to erect a Royal Arch just outside their building south of the City Hall and on the Royal couple's route as they were paraded through the city.

The IOF, which now operates out of a large building near the corner of Eglinton and Don Mills Road, has a most interesting history. While the Canadian 'court' was first established in London, Ontario, in 1876 and moved to our city in 1889, its genesis goes back to the days of King Richard II of England (1377–99). A group of men who guarded his forests formed a guild of Royal Foresters to protect both their rights and families.

In 1745, the Ancient Order of Foresters was created and, using some of the principles set out by the Royal Foresters, established an organization that provided assistance for widows and orphans through a scheme of cooperative life insurance.

In 1864, the Order crossed the Atlantic with the first U.S. court set up in Brooklyn. Soon, however, the Americans wanted their independence from the mother court in England. The IOF was born in Newark, N.J., in 1874.

The IOF arch (pictured above at its Ex site) was moved there in 1902 from its original location in the Bay-Richmond intersection (bottom).

A PIECE OF TORONTO SINCE 1922

December 1, 1985

The marquee on the Palais Royale ballroom advertises Toronto's popular
Ellis McLintock Orchestra in the late 1940s. *(THC)*

Recently I was asked to address guests at a Toronto Historical Board plaque
unveiling at the Palais Royale dance hall down at Sunnyside. In doing so I
thought it would be interesting to take a look at the year 1922 when the Palais
opened.

There was no television, and radio was little more than a toy. Nevertheless,
let's take a quick look through the *Evening Telegram* ... it's only two cents ... and
see what was happening.

In 1922 Canadian-born Andrew Bonar Law became premier of Great Britain
following the resignation of Lloyd George, while in the deserts of Egypt,
George Molyneaux and Howard Carter discovered the tomb of the young King
Tutankhamen, untouched since Tut's death in 1350 B.C. In that same year, oil
was discovered in Venezuela and in England the BBC was organized. On the
country's newsstands three new magazines appeared for the first time: *Reader's
Digest, True Confessions* and *Better Homes and Gardens.* Another magazine,
Physical Culture, announced that former ninety-seven-pound weakling, Angelo
Siciliano, had won the title of "the world's most perfectly developed man."
Angelo immediately changed his name ... to Charles Atlas.

The one-year-old Lincoln Motor Car Company was acquired by Edsel Ford
and the new $348 Star automobile was introduced in direct competition with

48

Ford's Model T. A price war resulted. To help pay for any bumps or dents in your new car, State Farm Automobile Insurance Company was formed selling policies only to clients whose cars were fully paid for.

At the movies Douglas Fairbanks, the husband of Toronto's own Mary Pickford, was carving a name for himself in *Robin Hood* and Rudolph Valentino kept them speechless in *Blood and Sand*. The world's first shopping centre, the Kansas City Country Club Shopping Plaza, opened in Kansas City, Mo., while in New York City, the hotel with the world's most famous telephone number, Pennsylvania 6-5000, the 2,200-room Hotel Pennsylvania, opened on Seventh Avenue. In 1922 a new word entered the advertisers' dictionary — halitosis — and helped boost sales of Listerine. In that same year Pep breakfast cereal hit the grocery shelves and Eskimo Pies made their first appearance.

On Wednesday, June 28th
at 8 o'clock
There will be opened for Toronto's Smart Set a magnificent pleasure palace on Sunnyside Promenade.

The Palais Royale
offering
Dancing, Refreshments and the
Wonderful Midnight Frolic
featuring
Harris and Kimmey
Late stars of Geo. M. Cohan's Broadway success "Mary."
and
Miss Lillian Bernard
Direct from the opening of Chicago's new palace, The Rainbow Garden.

Dancing	Refreshments	Midnight Frolic
8 to 11 p.m.	à la carte.	Supper Dance, 11 p.m. Phone Parkdale
10c a dance.	Highest quality	7165 for Reservations.

Come to the Palais Royale and Dance to the Melodies of the Million Dollar Orchestra.

Closer to home, medical researchers Frederick Banting and Charles Best gave their new diabetic treatment to Leonard Thompson at Toronto General Hospital. Thompson was given a new lease on life and insulin, called "iseltin" by Banting, became a godsend to thousands of diabetics around the world. Further downtown at City Hall, the politicians were demanding something to be done with ... wait for it ... the railway lands, though in 1922 they hadn't thought about a domed stadium yet. They were simply trying to get the federal government to approve construction of a badly needed cross-waterfront railway viaduct so they could use the new Union Station that had been completed two years earlier. Nothing happened and the station sat unused for another five years.

In March of '22 the *Toronto Star* broadcast the country's first live entertainment program over station 9AH and several months later went into the broadcasting business with their own station CFCA ("Canada's finest covers all"). Later that year the very first edition of the Royal Agricultural Winter Fair opened in the new Coliseum building at the Exhibition grounds, a structure that, at the time, had the largest amount of space under one roof in the world.

On the city's western waterfront, the new Sunnyside Amusement Park had just closed after a successful first year of operation. Sunnyside had been built and was administered by the Toronto Hydro Commission and was popularly known as "the poor man's Riviera." Its many rides, games and fast food stands provided a magical, mystical, musical retreat for Torontonians in 1922. One of the first structures erected at the new waterfront playground was a combination dance hall boat-building factory. Called the Palais Royale upstairs and Dean's Boat works downstairs, work on the $80,000 building began in 1921 and on June 28, 1922, it opened with a "wonderful Midnight Frolic" featuring, direct from George M. Cohan's Broadway musical, *Mary*, those two dancing, singing wizards, Harris and Kimmey, accompanied by the lovely Miss Lillian Bernard, recently the pride of Chicago's new entertainment palace, the Rainbow Garden.

Down below, under the dancing feet, Walter Dean, who had moved over from his old factory south of Lakeshore Road near the foot of Roncesvalles Avenue, was busily building his famous Sunnyside Torpedo canoe. Later that evening, it cost twelve cents a dance to glide around the hardwood floor to the melodies of the Palais' Million Dollar Orchestra.

Over the years the Palais became an immensely popular place competing with the nearby Sea-Breeze and Palace Pier, the Silver Slipper over on the Humber and just across the Lake Shore, the Club Esquire — later to be renamed the Top Hat. Radio and TV personality Elwood Glover reminisced about the Palais in my book *I Remember Sunnyside* with these words:

"I remember Cuthbert and Deller's Palais Royale with Bert Niosi's band playing nightly, a veritable magnet that drew me to every visiting name band that played there — at least one every two weeks in the late '30s: Basie, Ellington, Teagarden, Bob Crosby and Glen Gray. Imagine, in August of 1938, four straight nights of Artie Shaw's band. He was plugging a new record he'd just cut, 'Begin the Beguine.'"

Today only the recently restored Sunnyside Bathing pavilion and the Palais Royale remain as tangible reminders of a time when Torontonians enjoyed a red hot and a glass of Vernor's ginger ale followed by rides on the Flyer or Derby Racer and later, if you were lucky, a spin around the Palais' dance floor to the music of Bert Niosi or Ellis McLintock.

WHO WILL SAVE
OUR OLDEST HOUSE?

August 31, 1986

Toronto's oldest house is in trouble.

Nestled under the trees at the west end of the Exhibition grounds is the tiny Scadding cabin. Here's the story.

The province of Upper Canada was established by the British government in 1791 (hmmm ... there's a bicentennial coming) as a safe haven for those living in the rebellious States south of the

Scadding's cabin beside the Don River.

border who wished to remain loyal to King George III following the Revolutionary War.

This new political entity's first lieutenant-governor was one John Graves Simcoe, a prominent military gentleman and a clever statesman. When Simcoe departed England for his new command, he was accompanied by John Scadding, who had managed Simcoe's extensive farm in County Devon.

Soon after arriving at the future site of Toronto, Scadding was granted 250 acres of land on the east bank of the Don River fronting on the bay and running north as far as the concession road now known as Danforth Avenue. The east boundary of his property was a road allowance originally called Scadding Avenue. We now know it as Broadview Avenue.

In 1794, on the southern part of the property, south of what was the Kingston Road, the road to Kingston, and is now Queen Street. Scadding built a small cabin. However, within a couple of years, Simcoe was recalled to England and his faithful employee decided to return with him.

George Playter then moved into the house and in 1819 sold the fifty acres south of the Kingston Road to William Smith, Jr., who in turn gave the property and the buildings to his son John.

It was John Smith who in 1879 offered the historic cabin, built some forty-five years earlier by John Scadding to the officials of the newly organized Toronto Industrial Exhibition. In August of that year, eighteen members of the York Pioneer's Society assembled and, using an oxcart loaned by William Lea of Leaside, physically moved the structure from the banks of the Don, along King Street to its present location just west of the CNE Bandshell. To this day, the York Pioneer and Historical Society continues to look after the precious little building.

Now, the dedicated Pioneers need help.

ORIGINAL PINE UNDER ATTACK

Some of the original white pine logs have become infested with carpenter ants, and $15,000 is needed quickly to remedy a situation which, if left uncorrected, will destroy our city's oldest house.

Readers who might like to help are urged to contact the Pioneers at P.O. Box 481, Station K, Toronto M4P 2G9.

Thanks to the readers, enough money was collected to correct the problem.

An ironic sidebar to the Scadding story is the fact that John Scadding returned to York (now Toronto) in 1821 and spent years roughing it in the wilderness that has become Toronto. He came to an untimely end on March 1, 1824, at age sixty-nine, when a tree being cut down on his property near the present Don Jail fell on him.

York Pioneers on the way to erect their log house in Exhibition Park, Toronto, August 22, 1879.

A CENTURY OF MUSICAL MEMORIES

December 28, 1986

One of the landmark institutions in our city is celebrating its centennial this year.

Incorporated in 1886, the Royal Conservatory of Music (originally known as the Toronto Conservatory of Music) was the creation of Edward Fisher, among others, who was born in Vermont and came to Ottawa Ladies' College.

Several years later, he moved to Toronto where he became the organist at the four-year-old St. Andrew's Church on King Street West at Simcoe.

Though incorporated in 1886, the Conservatory didn't open until the following year and when it did so, it started simply, occupying two floors over a music store at the corner of Yonge and Wilton streets (now Yonge and Dundas Square).

Called the Toronto Conservatory of Music until 1947, this was the institution's home at the corner of University Avenue and College Street. A great deal of artistic licence was taken in preparing this sketch.

In its first year, the facility's fifty teachers offered some 200 students instruction in practical and theoretical music, as well as elocution, foreign languages, public school music, acoustics, piano-tuning, vocal anatomy and hygiene.

Up until 1893, teachers offered only guitar, saxophone and zither instruction.

In 1896 the Conservatory became affiliated with the University of Toronto and, in the following year, moved to a new home at the southwest corner of University and College streets — a site now occupied by the Ontario Hydro's head office.

It was about this time that the Conservatory established branch schools around Toronto and, by 1912, more than 2,000 students were enrolled in the system.

Over the ensuing years, the Conservatory became more closely affiliated with the University and more and more influential in the field of music throughout the country — so much so that on August 1, 1947, King George VI gave his consent to a change in the institution's name from the Toronto Conservatory to the Royal Conservatory of Music.

Five years later, the School of Music and Faculty of Music were created — the former to teach and examine and the latter to offer degrees and teaching diplomas.

Having outgrown the University and College buildings, the Faculty of Music moved to the new Edward Johnson Building on the University grounds in 1962 with the School of Music moving to the former McMaster University Building on Bloor Street West at Bedford in 1963.

Today, more than 100,000 students in Canada, the United States, West Germany and the Far East are enrolled in the various courses offered by our very own Royal Conservatory of Music.

Happy 100th!

GROWING CONGREGATION

January 25, 1987

Located at the southeast corner of King and Simcoe Streets in the heart of Toronto is the lovely old St. Andrew's Presbyterian Church which has graced that particular corner for more than a century.

In fact, the congregation of St. Andrew's is one of the oldest in our city having been established in 1830 and worshipping in their first church which was located at the southwest corner of Church and Adelaide streets. This building eventually proved to be too small for the growing congregation and a new structure was erected in the west-end of town.

Actually, the majority of members condoned the move to the new church, but a few wished to remain downtown and so the congregation split. The "old" St. Andrew's then became home to a very small congregation that eventually decided that it, too, would move. Thus it was that in 1878, two years after the "new" St. Andrew's opened at King and Simcoe, the "old" St. Andrew's moved to a brand new edifice at the southeast corner of Jarvis and Carlton streets.

An artist's impression of St. Andrew's and the new Symphony Place, an eighty-unit condominium.

That's why today there are two St. Andrew's Presbyterian churches in downtown Toronto, and it's also why the "old" St. Andrew's on Jarvis is younger, by two years, than the "new" St. Andrew's on King.

Incidentally, the St. Andrew's at King and Simcoe is about to take on a new look. Work will soon commence on a new eighty-unit condominium that will rise over the church manse located just south of the church.

Called Symphony Place, obviously for its proximity to Roy Thomson Hall across the street, this new structure will add another "ation" to what for a century has been called the four nations corner. On the site of Roy Thomson Hall was the lieutenant-governor's residence which was nicknamed legislation. On the north side of King was, until 1892, Upper Canada College — education; and across Simcoe, the British Tavern — damnation. The church was, of course, and still is, salvation. Soon we will be able to add to legislation, education, salvation and damnation, a fifth — habitation.

The actual date of this photo is estimated to be in 1885. It shows one of the early horse-cars of the Toronto Street Railway Company heading west along King Street in front of St. Andrew's Presbyterian Church.

NOW THAT'S ENTERTAINMENT ON THE VAUDEVILLE SCENE

February 8, 1987

Members of Toronto's social set were out in force that cold Monday night in mid-February, seventy-three years ago. It was opening night at the city's newest vaudeville house, the Winter Garden.

This new theatre was unique in that it had been built right on top of the recently opened Loew's Theatre on Yonge Street, just north of Queen. Called cleverly enough, Loew's Yonge Street, it had a seating capacity of 2,000 and opened on December 15, 1913, the latest addition to the chain of movie and vaudeville houses owned by theatrical impresario Marcus Lowe.

Christmas shoppers crowd Yonge Street in 1922 in front of Loew's where "At the Stage Door" and select vaudeville acts helped "pack 'em in." Just two doors south, the Red Mill Theatre carried on gamefully.

One of the guests of honour that December evening was a singing waiter turned songwriter. Young Israel Baline had arrived in America from his Russian homeland and changed his name to one that remains recognizable seven decades later ... Irving Berlin.

With Loew's off and running, workers turned to completing a second theatre high above the first. The Winter Garden, complete with apple blossoms, roses and leaves covering the walls and ceilings, tree trunks projecting from the sides of the stage and painted pastoral scenes everywhere, opened on February 16, 1914, with "dainty singer and dancer" Polly Prim as headliner.

Actually Polly shared the billing with Maurice Samuel and Company who performed in a play titled *A Day at Ellis Island* and the Moffatt, La Reine and Company who exhibited the wonder of the ages ... *X-Rays*.

Over the next few years, the same vaudeville bills were seen at both the downstairs and upstairs theatres, with the only difference being that seats could be reserved in the Winter Garden where the admission prices were slightly higher at 35¢, 45¢ and 50¢. Performers such as Sophie Tucker, Milton Berle, George Burns, Gracie Allen and Edgar Bergen entertained Torontonians in both Loew's and Winter Garden theatres.

By mid-1928, just fourteen years after the Winter Garden opened, both the theatre and vaudeville were redundant. Talkies were the rage. The Winter Garden closed. Downstairs Loew's dropped all its vaudeville in favour of talkies in 1930. Stripped of much of its grandeur with the arrival of Cinemascope in 1950, its name changed to the Yonge in 1970 and then to the Elgin in 1978.

Three years later, unable to complete outstanding work orders, the owners of the Elgin closed the theatre. A few weeks later the Ontario Heritage Foundation purchased the structure and work started on plans to restore the old Elgin and Winter Garden theatres, both of which had been designated as National Historic Sites.

Then in 1984, the city's Sesquicentennial Year and after a couple of aborted starts, restoration of the Elgin commenced with the removal of twenty-five coats of paint from the lobby colonnades. Then, on March 14, 1985, a menagerie of felines moved in. Exactly two years later on the evening of this coming March 14, 1987, all the cats will move out. With purr-fect timing, a very special last night performance of *CATS* will kick off a major fund-raising program to restore the tarnished, yet still spectacular, Winter Garden.

RADIO STATION CELEBRATES
BROADCASTING MIRACLE

February 15, 1987

Radio whiz young Edward Samuel Rogers.

The nineteenth of this month marks the sixtieth anniversary of an event that occurred in the history of radio broadcasting that was to have far-reaching effects, not only here in Toronto, but worldwide as well.

It was on February 19, 1927, that a young Edward Samuel Rogers (called Ted and the father of Ted Rogers, Jr., owner of this station and CFTR) introduced Torontonians (at least to those who could afford to own a radio) to his new radio station with the now famous call sign CFRB. It was then positioned at 1030 on the dial and broadcasted from studios in the old Massey mansion on Jarvis Street which is now the Keg restaurant.

While it's true the station began broadcasting that cold Saturday night in mid-February, the twenty-seven-year-old man who had dreamt it up had spent much of his life experimenting with the newest miracle in the golden age of communication ... wireless radio.

Ted Rogers was born in Toronto in 1900, the son of a well-to-do business-man and a relative of the well-known Elias Rogers.

As a child, Ted was fascinated with amateur radio. Several rooms in his father's Rosedale home at 9 Nanton Avenue were filled with equipment and bulky storage batteries. The latter items were the scourge of the radio enthusiast because of their size, unreliability and safety (sulphuric acid being a necessary component).

Reading about some experiments that were going on in the States whereby alternating current was used to replace the batteries, Rogers acquired the Canadian rights to the experimental AC tube.

Working long hours in a small lab on Chestnut Street, Rogers perfected his AC tube and soon began building radios, without the batteries, that gave reception that was clearer and better than ever before possible.

Even though Toronto was served by five radio stations at that time, Rogers decided to develop one using the "batteryless principle" found in his radios.

So it was on the evening of February 19, 1927, sixty years ago, history was made and CFRB, "Canada's first Rogers' Batteryless," went on the air.

Just twelve years later, Ted Rogers was dead at the age of thirty-nine. His legacy lives on.

Now a Keg restaurant, the former Massey mansion was the site of
CFRB's first studio in 1927.

SOME SUPERHIGHWAY HISTORY

October 11, 1987

It's frequently jammed so badly that you can't use it, but nevertheless, it's hard to imagine where we'd be without it. What's the *it* I'm talking about? The good old Queen Elizabeth Highway, that's what.

And I mean no disrespect when I call it old. Nevertheless, in terms of the modern superhighway, the QEW will soon be fifty and, when compared to other superhighways, fifty is old.

The first of the QEW-type thoroughfares was constructed between Milan and Varese in Italy in the mid-1920s, followed almost a decade later by the German autobahns that Hitler was soon to put to a special use. At about the same time, on this side of the Atlantic Ocean, American engineers were focusing their efforts on what they called "parkways." These parkways had fundamentally different purposes than the autobahns in that the parkways were built to get traffic in and out of large cities rather than convey traffic between large cities as in Europe.

In fact, by the time the first American version of the autobahn — the Pennsylvania Turnpike — opened in October of 1940, we here in Canada had been using our very own "autobahn," the Queen Elizabeth Highway for more than a year.

Work started on the QEW in the spring of 1931 when several dozen out-of-work laborers began widening a thoroughfare called the Middle Road. It was a narrow, unpaved country road joining Toronto and Hamilton almost midway between two other thoroughfares — the Lakeshore Road and the old Dundas Highway now called No. 5. Actually, the Middle Road was simply an extension of Toronto's Queen Street on the west side of the Humber River.

Over the years, it had become obvious to officials of the province's highways department that something had to be done about the overcrowding on the Lakeshore and Dundas highways. That was a result of the spectacular increase in inter-city highway traffic between Toronto and Hamilton following the end of the First War. That lead to a new highway called "the Queen Street Extension."

The first section of the new highway was the stretch between the old Brown's Line (now Highway 427) and the Port Credit-Cooksville Road (now Highway 10). Then in 1934, construction plans were revised and what started out as just another highway became a "super-highway," featuring four lanes of traffic, wider traffic lanes, higher vehicle speeds, limited access to and from the highway and for the first time in Canada a cloverleaf whereby Highway 10 would be carried over the new Middle Road Highway. Work on the cloverleaf interchange began in 1937.

While work continued on extending the new super-highway from Toronto's doorstep west to Burlington and Hamilton, provincial officials made the dramatic decision to continue the thoroughfare all the way to Niagara Falls and to the lucrative American tourist market just across the Niagara River. Much controversy arose when lush Niagara Peninsula farmland was sacrificed for a highway

Canada's first cloverleaf under construction in 1937 at the soon-to-be QEW and Highway 10. Same interchange (below) in 1983.

that permitted people to drive from the Falls to Hamilton in just thirty minutes. Nevertheless, work continued and on June 7, 1939, near the Henley Bridge at St. Catharines, a deep crimson Buick convertible carrying King George VI and his Queen, who were in the midst of their first ever Canadian visit, broke a light beam that caused two huge Union Jacks to part revealing the thoroughfare's new name, The Queen Elizabeth Highway.

Now the highway had a name, but it still wasn't complete. That didn't happen for another fourteen and a half months when on August 23, 1940, the provincial highways minister and the man most responsible for the construction of the highway, Thomas McQuesten, performed the honours at the beautiful Henley bridge across the Twelve Mile Bridge at St. Catharines.

The last four-lane stretch of the QEW that joins Niagara Falls and Fort Erie, a section that still looks much like the highway was first destined to look, wasn't completed until the fall of 1956.

For more on the QEW, read Robert Stamp's new book *QEW. Canada's First Superhighway* (Boston Mills Press). It's available for $9.95 from Longhouse Books on Yonge Street in Toronto, or from the publisher ($9.95 postage paid) at 132 Main Street, Erin, Ontario N0B 1T0.

To the reader asking about the proper spelling of a street running east off Broadview, south off Danforth, *Woolfrey* as on the building or *Wolfrey* as on the street sign, the former, according to the 1893 city directory, is correct.

HISTORIAN
DOCUMENTED MEMORIES
Master of Toronto of Old

February 14, 1988

Tucked in-between the massive Eaton Centre complex and the historic Holy Trinity Church is a three-storey structure that dates from 1857. Now officially referred to as #10 Trinity square, the structure's best-known resident was Dr. Henry Scadding, without doubt this city's greatest historian.

It's thanks to this gentleman that we know so much of our great city's early history; and in tribute to Henry Scadding's love for his city and it's history, the building is now known as Scadding House.

Scadding was born in England in 1813, the youngest son of John and Milicent Scadding. As a young man Scadding, Sr., had worked for John Simcoe as property manager, overseeing Simcoe's 5,000 acre estate near Wolford in Devonshire.

When Simcoe was appointed lieutenant-governor of the newly created Province of Upper Canada in 1791, his young assistant decided to accompany his boss to the "new world."

King Street, looking east, as it would have appeared during the days Henry Scadding was growing up.

Then Simcoe decided to move the young province's capital from Newark (Niagara-on-the-Lake) to a "temporary" location (actually at this time, not much more than a clearing in the dense forest) on the other side of the lake, well distant from the American border. John Scadding, along with others who agreed to join the lieutenant-governor in developing the new townsite, was given a substantial land grant on the east bank of the Don River stretching from Toronto Bay north to the Second Concession, today's Danforth Avenue.

Simcoe's "temporary" capital has evolved into today's modern Metropolitan Toronto.

When ill health forced Simcoe to return to England in1796, Scadding accompanied him, and once again took up the position of estate manager in Devonshire; first for the ex-lieutenant-governor and after his death in 1806, for his wife, Elizabeth.

It was shortly before John Simcoe died that Scadding met and married Milicent Triggs. She presented him with three sons, the youngest being Henry. When the youngster was but eight years of age, the Scadding family returned to Upper Canada taking up residence on the same land grant given to Scadding, Sr., by Simcoe twenty-nine years before.

One of the original Scadding buildings, that used to stand on the east bank of the Don (just north of Queen Street), now stands in the CNE grounds.

Three years after their return to Upper Canada John Scadding was killed when a tree fell on him.

Henry Scadding got the best primary education available in the young community and was the first pupil to enrol in the newly established Upper Canada College that opened at the corner of King and Simcoe streets in 1830. He completed his education at St. John's College, Cambridge, receiving a Doctorate of Divinity in 1852.

Scadding returned to Toronto in 1838, was appointed a classical master at Upper Canada College and after being ordained a minister and serving a short time as assistant minister at St. James, he became the first rector of the newly consecrated Holy Trinity Church.

In 1849, he helped establish the Royal Canadian Institute. Scadding retired from UCC in 1862 and from Holy Trinity in 1875. Five years later he was elected president of the York Pioneer and Historical Society (still a very active organization), a position he held for eighteen years. Henry Scadding died at his residence, #10 Trinity Square, in 1901.

One of the elderly gentleman's greatest pleasures was documenting his memories of an earlier Toronto. Scadding contributed descriptive text to John Charles Dent's *Toronto, Past and Present* (published in 1894) and Mercer Adam's *Toronto Old and New* (1891) both of these books are much sought after by collectors.

Recently, Dundurn Press of Toronto has reprinted Scadding's own masterpiece on Toronto's early history. First published in 1873 (original copies are now worth in the vicinity of $100) *Toronto of Old* continues to bring the city of the early 1830s to life as the accomplished writer/researcher/ raconteur wanders the streets of the little town and paints for the reader a vivid picture of York as it approached 1834, the year the small community was elevated to city status. Thanks to Dundurn Press, this popular-priced edition makes it available reading for all.

Dr. Henry Scadding, author of *Toronto of Old.*

FOREST LAWN MAUSOLEUM
Entombed in Tranquility

October 23, 1988

Some of T.O.'s prominent citizens rest here.

Motorists frequenting the Yonge and Highway 401 part of the city have, no doubt, seen the two large concrete-block buildings tucked in behind a vine-covered fence on the west side of Yonge Street. The structures are just north of the 401 interchange and across from the Maclean Hunter plant.

Called the Forest Lawn Mausoleum, the complex is made up of several newer and smaller structures than the two original concrete-block buildings. The older structures are virtually identical from the exterior, although constructed six years apart. Inside, the walls and foyer are lined with beautiful white marble and form the exterior of hundreds of above-ground crypts. There are also several "private rooms" containing crypts, each identified with the name of the deceased, dates of birth and death, and a short epitaph. The setting is both solemn and breathtaking.

But to fully appreciate the story, let's go back in time and look at the early history of Forest Lawn. Early this century, a company called the International Mausoleum Company, with offices at 88 Victoria Street, was organized. Appointed as directors were well-known Torontonians such as, Sir Henry (Casa Loma) Pellatt, S. Morley Wickett of Wickett and Craig tanners, and lawyer Miller Lash.

In those days, many of the city's prominent citizens had a preference to be buried "above ground" rather than "under ground." While most of the existing cemeteries around town had provisions for both types of burials, Forest Lawn was to be developed to provide, exclusively, "above ground" burials in large crypts.

Initial plans called for sixteen large mausoleum structures on 132-acres in the Village of Lansing, Ontario (today's Yonge and Sheppard area). It was a community located a mile or so north of the city limits and accessible by motor car via Yonge Street or by streetcar on the Toronto and York Radial Railway's Metropolitan line. The line operated from the new North Toronto CPR Station, just south of St. Clair Avenue, all the way up Yonge to Aurora, then across country to Newmarket, Jackson's Point and Sutton.

In those days, many of the city's best-known citizens had country properties north of the city. So the idea that following their death, relatives and friends had easy access to the mausoleum via the big green radial cars, was probably an appealing selling feature.

Initial plans called for a complex of sixteen structures scattered throughout the property. In the architects' concept above (kindly loaned to me by the present owners of Forest Lawn), we can see, in addition to the two buildings actually built, thirteen other structures situated in a semi-circle with the largest building of them all sitting mid semi-circle. Tree-lined pathways were to interconnect the complex of sixteen mausoleums.

To get the project off the ground, the first structure was built at the north end of the property in 1911. A second, smaller building was added to the south in 1917. Then for various reasons, the company's grand scheme was abandoned.

Meanwhile, some of T.O.'s more prominent citizens resting at Forest Lawn include Sir Henry Pellatt; William Neilson, of chocolate fame; former Mayor Emerson Coatsworth; and several Torontonians who lost their lives when the liner Lusitania sunk May 7, 1915.

Forest Lawn is owned by Westside Cemeteries Ltd., which also owns Sanctuary Park and Riverside Cemeteries in Weston, and Innisfil Mausoleum near Barrie.

Architects' original concept for the massive Forest Lawn Mausoleum complex in Lansing, Ontario. Only the two buildings (identified by arrows) were built.

PUTTING TORONTO ON THE MAP

November 6, 1988

The redevelopment of downtown Toronto goes on and on. One faction at City Hall gives thumbs up to virtually anything that comes along — in spite of all the warnings by experts. Meanwhile, the other side turns thumbs down on these same projects.

So far, there are more thumbs up than down and the traffic gets worse.

One day, while perusing some documents in the City Archives down in the basement of New City Hall, I came across a redevelopment proposal put forward by an American company, United Engineering and Construction Company. The company's head office was located in Los Angeles and their Canadian office, run by Andrew J. Little, was in a small office on the second floor of the Confederation Life Building at Yonge and Richmond streets.

In September of 1911, United Engineering approached the City's Board of Control with a proposal to build a huge — and I mean huge — structure occupying the entire area bounded by Yonge, King, York and Queen streets. Almost sixty acres. The mammoth structure would burrow three storeys below ground and tower twenty storeys above ground. In total, the "Toronto Union Terminal and Commercial Building" would provide 1,000 acres or 40 million square feet of space (as a reference point, the recently approved $500 million Bay-Adelaide Court project is only 2 million square feet or five percent of this idea). This massive terminal would serve the country's three transcontinental railways, a gigantic hotel, rows of retail stores, several hundred business offices, numerous theatres and a cache of banks. And, to quote from the prospectus, provisions for "all lines known to the commercial world." The prospectus goes on: "Even at $1 per square foot rental, it will pay substantial revenue."

In this same prospectus, the development company offered a solution to the city's railway problem: Have all trains enter the heart of the city in long tunnels, thereby removing all tracks from city streets. Railway tracks, over which pedestrian and vehicular traffic had to cross to get to and from the harbour, had been an ongoing headache for the city fathers ever since the first steam train chugged out of town in 1853.

By the turn of the century, steam tracks in downtown Toronto was one enormous problem. The federal government finally ordered the construction of a cross-waterfront railway viaduct, which opened in the late '20s. Therefore, in retrospect, one can see how welcomed United Engineering's proposal might have been to both city politicians and a public concerned about deteriorating safety conditions.

Another selling feature of the proposal was the plan to use the earth excavated from the below-ground phase to fill and improve the city's waterfront. This was in anticipation of the huge ocean-going freighters and passenger liners that would arrive upon completion of a deep waterway canal through the St. Lawrence Valley (the St. Lawrence Seaway wasn't operational for another four decades).

In the drawing accompanying the proposal (below) sailing ships and multi-funnelled passenger vessels, like the White Star line's Olympic, are moored alongside four massive wharves. And, who knows, they may have been thinking about the arrival someday of Olympic's sister ship. At the time of this 1911 proposal, the ship, under the company designation SS400, was still in the Belfast shipyard of Harland and Wolff being fitted out. SS400 would never make it to this side of the Atlantic — let alone to the Port of Toronto. On April 15, 1912, RMS *Titanic* struck an iceberg and sank igniting a flame of controversy that still burns.

The method of financing United Engineering's project is interesting. The proposal suggested that the numerous land and building owners occupying the site, put their property in on a stock-ownership basis. United company also suggested various local building materials companies wanted stock in the project instead of cash payments.

To quote the proposal: "It is not too colossal an enterprise for Canada's Queen City to undertake to place herself on record before the world centres of doing things. In the advanced events of today, ranking among the survival of the fittest, to whom the better part of the world belongs, Toronto will surely show them; then keep your eye on Toronto."

Nevertheless, in spite of all the hoopla, the plan died at the Board of Control. Thank Goodness.

Bird's-eye view of Toronto showing the proposed mammoth Toronto Union and Commercial Building, bounded by Yonge, Queen, York and King streets. *(CTA)*

TRACING "T.O." STREET NAMES

December 18, 1988

Metro's Eglinton Avenue takes its name from Prestwick's historic
Eglinton Castle.

As the old year draws to a close, I'd like to recount one of my major accomplishments of '88. In September, I finally made it over to Great Britain. While my wife and I have visited the continent on a couple of occasions, we had never made it to England. But accompanied by our good friends Joy and Dave Garrick, we finally did it. And the experience was great!

A quick look at any Metro street map reveals a great many of the street names are taken from places in England. One of the reasons for the trip was to compile additional material for a book I'm doing on the origins of Toronto street names.

One of our first stops? Tracking down the origin of Toronto's Eglinton Avenue.

A few miles north of Prestwick is the small community of Irvine and nearby one can find the ruins of Eglinton Castle. It was here in 1839, the twenty-six-year-old 13th Earl of Eglinton, Archibald William Montgomerie, held a mock medieval-style tournament, complete with jousting, feasting and carousing.

Dozens from the ranks of the nobility attended, as did thousands of the not-so-noble. Word of the remarkable event spread far and wide, and it is quite likely early settlers, in what is now the North Toronto area of our city, also heard about it. There, in the midst of fields and forests, they probably decided, albeit tongue-in-cheek, that this part of the world would be their Eglinton.

The next day we were in the beautiful city of Edinburgh. Just off Princess Street is a towering monument commemorating the first Viscount Melville, Sir Henry Dundas. In addition to holding several other titles, the Viscount was the secretary of state in the cabinet of King George III, the reigning monarch during our city's formative years. Nearby is the former residence of the Viscount, now stunningly restored. Using the Viscount's surname, Toronto's founder, John Simcoe, named one of his young community's original thoroughfares Dundas Street.

T.O.'s Bathurst Street is named after a past relative of Henry Bathurst (right), the 8th Earl Bathurst, posing with pet, Jamie.

On the way from Edinburgh to the English border is the small town of Melrose. One of the community's best-known citizens was poet and novelist Sir Walter Scott. When the lands in north Toronto were being developed in 1910, one of Sir Walter's fans, who worked for the Robins real estate company, selected the name Melrose Park for the new subdivision. And Melrose Avenue was assigned to the narrow thoroughfare through the farm fields abutting the west side of a dusty road called Yonge Street.

In Yorkshire, on the North Sea coastline, is the bustling Town of Scarborough (surrounded by Towns of Whitby, Pickering, Malton and Filey). This Yorkshire town was visited several times by the wife of Upper Canada's first lieutenant-governor. Years later, Elizabeth Simcoe visited the future site of Toronto with her husband, John Simcoe. So impressed was she with the bluffs to the east of her husband's newly established Town of York and their similarity to the bluffs at Scarborough in England, that she named both the bluffs and a new township after the English Scarborough.

In the lake district of the County of Shropshire and close to the Welsh border is the old market town of Ellesmere. While the suffix "mere" means lake, historians are unsure as to the origins of the prefix. Metro's Ellesmere Road comes from the early settlement of Ellesmere that grew around the present Ellesmere-Kennedy Road intersection in the mid-1800s. Early settlers from Ellesmere in England brought the name of their hometown with them, and gave it to the new settlement to lessen the unfriendliness of the strange and desolate surroundings.

Almost due south of Ellesmere in the County of Devonshire is the final resting place of our province's first lieutenant-governor, his wife, Elizabeth and five of their eleven children. The story of Wolford Chapel will be the subject of another "The Way We Were" column. However, a few miles east of the chapel in beautiful Dorsetshire, is another town whose name has been transferred, albeit with a slight spelling change, to one of Toronto's major downtown thoroughfares.

Sherborne has the air of a small cathedral city, with its numerous medieval buildings, superb Abbey Church, schools, almshouse and pair of castles. Its connection with our city evolves from the fact that Thomas Gibbs Ridout, a prominent Toronto businessman and managing director of the Bank of Upper Canada, acquired a large tract of land in Toronto from his half-brother, Samuel. He constructed a thoroughfare along the west boundary of his property and had it named Sherborne, after his father's birthplace in Dorsetshire, England. The spelling had, for some unknown reason been altered to the present spelling.

In the all-too-brief three days we were able to spend in London, I was able to visit Hammersmith and Kew, Islington and Soho, Kensington and Fleet, all others that have given their names to Toronto streets.

Memorial to the man after whom our Bathurst Street is named.

KEEPING THE SPIRITS ALIVE IN HISTORY BOOKS / GOODERHAM AND WORTS

August 26, 1990

This view of our city's shoreline shows the distillery in full production
late last century.

On the last day of this month, the city's oldest industry will close its doors forever. As of Friday, August 31, the venerable old distillery at the foot of Trinity Street operated by Gooderham and Worts for more than a century and a half will be no more. The reasons for the firm's demise here are both financial and political. Nevertheless, the bottom line is that another Toronto tradition has gone the way of the dodo (the bird, not any specific politician).

The Gooderham story begins in the year 1832 when James Worts and William Gooderham established a flour mill on the edge of the bay, between the east boundary of the Town of York (as Toronto was then called) and the River Don.

Worts had arrived in the little town the previous year from Suffolk, England, and began erecting a flour mill in a forest clearing east of today's Parliament Street. In 1832 he was joined by his brother-in-law, William Gooderham, who had also decided to emigrate to the young province of Upper Canada from his native England. Accompanying Gooderham on his voyage were members of both the Gooderham and Worts families, several of their servants and a total of eleven orphans. In all, the arrival of Gooderham and his retinue increased the town's population of 3,969 by fifty-four.

Gooderham invested three thousand pounds (approximately fifteen thousand dollars) in the new partnership which soon became known throughout the area as Worts and Gooderham. Their mill was unique in that it had a seventy-foot-high windmill constructed of red brick that stood on the edge of Toronto Bay. The windmill's large vanes were turned by gusts of wind that raced over the open expanse of Toronto Bay. Through a series of gears, this wind was used to run the grinding stone which in turn pulverized the grain from local farmers.

The last barrel of product leaves the G & W plant days before the old distillery closed on August 31, 1990. Office and plant staff signed the barrel before shipping it to British Columbia.

Because most farmers were used to paying for goods and services with quantities of grain, it wasn't long before this so-called "payment" was being converted into alcohol and sold. Eventually, the production of spirits overtook the milling of flour and in 1845, a new business called the Toronto Steam Mills and Distillery was born.

Unfortunately, one of the partners wasn't around when the new business came into being, for in February 1834, James Worts had committed suicide by throwing himself down the distillery well after hearing that his beloved wife (George Gooderham's sister) had died in childbirth.

Gooderham was now faced with the responsibility of not only running a very busy distilling business, but also looking after his own children, of which there were thirteen, plus those of his late brother-in-law. In 1845, Gooderham brought his nephew, James Gooderham Worts, into the business as a full partner and the company name was changed once more, this time to the well-known Gooderham and Worts.

As the years went by the enterprise continued to grow, and in 1877 it was boldly announced that Toronto's Gooderham and Worts Distillery was the largest in the world. Then, in 1923 the entire operation was sold to Canadian-born businessman Harry Hatch who merged the distillery with his Hiram Walker operation in Windsor, Ontario.

In more recent years, the entire Hiram Walker/Gooderham and Worts conglomerate came under the control of the Britain's Allied Lyons who have determined that the Toronto operation is redundant. As a result, at the end of this week, all operations at the 158-year-old plant, Toronto's oldest, will cease and the doors will be locked.

The future of the site and of the numerous historic buildings is unknown.

NAME THAT STREET

February 21, 1993

Clinton and Gore. They have theirs, we have ours.

South of the border the Clinton-Gore combination is still feeling its way around as the United States' new presidential team.

Here at home, the Clinton-Gore combo has been around for a century. In our case, however, the names refer to a street intersection in west-central Toronto.

Clinton Street first appeared in the city directories in the early 1870s and my guess is that it was named in honour of the British statesman, Henry Pelham Clinton, the fifth Duke of Newcastle, who was born in London, England, in 1811. He was educated in both Eton and Oxford following which he held numerous important government positions.

In 1859 this Clinton was appointed secretary of state for the Colonies, and while holding that office accompanied eighteen-year-old Prince Albert Edward, then the Prince of Wales (and the future King Edward VII), on his tour of Canada. in 1860. While in Toronto, the Prince dedicated both Queen's Park and the Horticultural Gardens (now Allan Gardens).

As the majority of the American voters said, "there's only one way to go, Clinton and Gore." Locally, Clinton and Gore are streets in west-central Toronto.

It's quite likely that as a result of the young Prince's immense popularity while in Toronto, civic officials paid it's respect to Clinton, or to use his official title, the Duke of Newcastle, who had been charged with the rather daunting responsibility of keeping an eye on a "frisky" young prince, by naming a new city street after him.

Henry Clinton died suddenly on October 18, 1864.

The origin of the name Gore for the little street that intersects Clinton, one block south of College Street, is a little easier to deduce.

Soon after the little community called York was established in 1793 (200 years ago!), substantial grants of land (100-acre Town Lots and 200-acre Park Lots) were awarded by Governor John Simcoe in the name of the Crown to deserving and loyal citizens in an effort to encourage development of the new townsite and its environs.

Simcoe returned to England in 1796 and in the years following his departure, land grants continued to be awarded to deserving applicants. One such grant, Park Lot 22, fronting on today's Queen Street and located about halfway between the modern north-south thoroughfares called Bathurst and Dufferin, was made in 1806 to Samuel Smith, a captain in Simcoe's military regiment, the Queen's Rangers. And, while Smith didn't build on the property, the captain did give it a name, "Gore," for the newly appointed lieutenant-governor of the young province, Francis Gore, and "vale" for the ravine that cut through the parcel of land.

Sir Francis Gore was to hold the position of lieutenant-governor of Upper Canada (Ontario) until 1817. He died in 1852.

Park Lot 22 was sold twice over the next few years, and in 1820 the third owner, Duncan Cameron, erected a large house on the property which he called Gore Vale.

Over the ensuing years, the house and ever-shrinking parcel of land surrounding it, was sold several more times coming into the possession of Edward Brickford, an influential railway contractor, in 1870.

It was inevitable that as the city continued to expand, the undeveloped area surrounding George Vale would be subdivided and streets and houses were built. Names for the new thoroughfares were needed and so it was that two of Brickford's daughters, Grace and Beatrice, became immortalized on street maps as did the name of the old family residence, though the street nomenclature became a single word, Gorevale.

As other streets in the area were laid out, more names were needed. One such thoroughfare, located north of Gorevale and east of both Beatrice and Grace, first appears in the city directories in 1893. It's a fairly safe assumption that it,too, was named in honour of the same Mr. Gore who was recognized in the term Gorevale.

FAMED COMIC HAS
CANADA CONNECTION

September 5, 1993

MM y favorite comedian's coming
"home" and he'll be at the
O'Keefe Centre this coming Friday
and Saturday, September 10th and
11th.

Sure, I know the record books tell
you that Red Skelton was born in
Indiana a whole bunch of years ago
(it's hard to believe he was eighty last
July 18), but what those same books
don't tell you is that it was while performing on the stages of theaters in
Montreal and Toronto that Red got
his first real break in show business.

Life was a challenge from the start
for the young Richard Red Skelton
(born with a full head of red hair, his
mother actually chose "Red" as the
baby's middle name) as it was for the
entire family, consisting of the matri-
arch, Ida Mae, Richard and his three
older brothers Paul, Denny and
Christopher.

While still in just grade three,
young Richard, now more frequently
referred to as Red, began selling

The legendary Red Skelton was
described as "the Canadian Comedian"
when he first hit the big time south of
the border.

newspapers on street corners with the money he made helping to support the
fatherless Skelton family, Joseph Skelton, a circus clown, having died just
months before Richard was born.

At the age of ten, Red got a job sweeping floors in a local poolroom followed
by a stint in the shipping room of a large department store in his hometown of
Vincennes. One day "Doc" Lewis's traveling medicine show arrived in town,
caught the youngster's fancy and soon Red was earning a dollar a week as the
show's new singing act. His remuneration began to climb (once he stopped
singing, Red claims) and by summer's end he was making ten times the figure
scribbled on his first cheque. He then joined the John Lawrence stock compa-

ny, followed the next year by a stint with the popular Clarence Stout Minstrels.

There was no doubt that Richard Red Skelton had definitely been bitten by the show bug.

After completing grade six, fourteen-year-old Red left school permanently to pursue his show business future on the famous showboat *Cotton Blossom* (curiously, a vessel with the same name is featured as "THE" showboat in Jerome Kern's musical debuting next month at the North York Performing Arts Centre) that plied the Mississippi and Ohio rivers. At the age of just sixteen, Red was reputed to be the youngest comedian in burlesque.

As the Great Depression took hold, things began to sour for the young comedian and work in show business became harder and harder to find. Soon Red found himself working outside the States for the first time, landing a job as a master of ceremonies on a vaudeville circuit that took in theaters in both Quebec and Ontario. He'd appear for a week on the stage of the Loew's Princess in Montreal followed by a week on the Shea's Hippodrome stage here

Red's Toronto "home" while in Toronto was the Ford Hotel at the northeast corner of Bay and Dundas streets. Opened in 1928 it was a nice enough place to stay in its early years, but slipped badly later, eventually being put out of its misery in 1973.

in Toronto. The Hippodrome had been a fixture on the west side of Teraulay Street (as Bay north of Queen was then called) since its opening in 1917. When the decision was made to build a new city hall and civic square

Ad for Red's hotel soon after it opened.

across from the city hall of the day, the fate of the theatre was sealed. The Hippodrome was demolished in 1956.

It was while Red worked in Canada, making the 338-mile CPR train ride between the two Canadian cities on a weekly basis, that he devised two of his most popular routines, the doughnut dunkers and the "mean, widdle kid," the former originating while Red ate in a Montreal diner and the latter during a visit to the Canadian National Exhibition where he witnessed a mother and her obnoxious child in an animated and heated confrontation.

Red's connection with Canada was so strong that when he finally returned to the States for a stint at the Capital theatre in Washington, D.C., he was billed as the "Canadian comedian," a description that Red still remembers with pride.

The rest, Skelton's radio, movie, television and stage career, are, as they say, things from which legends are made.

❧

During Red's last visit to Toronto I had the privilege of meeting him backstage. Being somewhat in awe as I stood in the presence of this show business legend, my first question to him was a rather stunned "where'd you stay while performing in Toronto?" Like he'd remember out of all the places he's stayed during his lengthy career the one here in Toronto he called home those many years ago.

Then, as if someone had prompted him that I was going to ask that somewhat inane question he shot back, without missing a beat, "why, the Ford Hotel."

Of course, that made all kinds of sense. The Ford was both handy (located as it was just up the street from Shea's at the northeast corner of Bay and Dundas) and it was still relatively new (having opened eight years before Red's 1936 stay in Toronto) and affordable.

In later years, its reputation began to suffer and in 1973 was demolished.

HISTORY AS THEATRE
200 TORONTO YEARS

As part of the community's bicentennial (Toronto was founded as York in 1793) the Toronto Sun commissioned local artist John Hood to create a mural on the Front Street East wall of the Sun Building. Here's the story of his mural.

Toronto artist John Hood has captured in this remarkable 180 foot (55 m.) long, 25 foot (7.6 m.) high mural, titled *HISTORY AS THEATRE, 200 TORONTO YEARS,* thirty-two vignettes highlighting both historic and contemporary episodes from the city's first two centuries. This work, which was completed in 1993, the community's bicentennial year, is presented as a "thank you" to all Torontonians who have helped "The Little Paper" grow.

(Refer to the outline key for individual historic vignettes (lettered) and specific people, buildings and objects (numbered) related to that vignette.)

John's mural is approaching the half-way mark in this June 23, 1993 photo.

VIGNETTE A: NATIVE CANADIANS, pre-history to 1759

For centuries before the arrival of the first European explorers and settlers the area destined to become the site of today's modern Metropolitan Toronto was heavily wooded, criss-crossed by clear-running streams and frequently traversed by Native Canadians, Ojibwa (1), Huron (2 & 3) and Iroquois (4). In fact, the name Toronto itself is believed by many to be derived from the native expression for *meeting place.*

VIGNETTE B: ETIENNE BRULE, 1615

In the early fall of 1615 French adventurer Etienne Brûlé (5), who explored much of the "New World" with his famous mentor, the legendary Samuel de Champlain, descended *le passage de Toronto* (now the Humber River) and from a promontory near its confluence with *Lac Ontario* became the first European to view the site of the future City of Toronto.
(6) Brûlé's Huron guide.

VIGNETTE C: FORT ROUILLE, 1750–59

A little more than a century after Brûlé paddled down the Humber River, the French government established the first of three trading posts in the Toronto area. In 1750 the third of these, named Fort Rouillé (10) in honour of the French Minister of Marine and Colonies and manned by members of Les Compagnies Franches de la Marine (7 & 8), was constructed near the site of the present bandshell in Exhibition Place. Trading between the French and Indians kept this palisaded structure a busy place until 1759 when escalating hostilities between the British and French resulted in the burning of the fort, now more commonly referred to as Fort Toronto, to prevent it from falling into the hands of the enemy.
(9) A French missionary's visitation to Fort Toronto.

VIGNETTE D: THE TORONTO PURCHASE, 1787 & 1805

On September 23, 1787, Lord Dorchester (15), Governor-in-Chief of Canada, arranged for the purchase of 250,880 acres of land from the Mississauga for the sum of £1,700 (approximately $8,500) plus some barrels of cloth, a few axes and a quantity of other small items. This transaction, which became known as *the Toronto Purchase,* included virtually all the land now covered by Metro Toronto. Present at the first meeting were three Mississauga chiefs including Wabukanyne (17, 18 & 19). However, due to several defects in the original document of sale, in was necessary to ratify the agreement at a subsequent ceremony held on board a British naval vessel on August 1, 1805. The latter event is depicted in this vignette and is based on a painting by C.W. Jefferys. British grenadier (11), British officer (12), Sir John Johnson, Superintendent of Indian Affairs (13), Colonel John Butler, American-born leader of Loyalist refugees (14), French interpreter (16), twelve-pound shipboard cannon (20).

VIGNETTE E: THE NAMING OF YORK, AUGUST 1793
(based on a passage from Elizabeth Simcoe's diary)

Following the establishment of the new Province of Upper Canada by the British government in 1791 (the province was renamed Ontario in 1867), John Graves Simcoe

(29) was appointed the province's first lieutenant-governor. Anticipating military action with Britain's foe, the United States of America, one of Simcoe's first acts as lieutenant-governor was to establish a naval shipyard on the north shore of Lake Ontario where armed vessels could be built. The site he selected was at the east end of the sheltered bay located a short distance east of the ruins of the old French fort. Before long a small community began to develop near the shipyard, a community that took as its name the Indian word long associated with the area, Toronto. Unappreciative of Indian words, Simcoe soon ordered that it be renamed York in honour of the Duke of York, second eldest son of Britain's King George III, with the ensuing ceremony, which occurred on August 27, 1793, depicted in this vignette.

Officer and soldiers (21, 22 & 30) of Simcoe's military regiment, the Queen's Rangers, Ojibwa men (23 & 26), Ojibwa chief Canise (24) carrying Simcoe's young son Francis (25) on his shoulders, (27) Simcoe's daughter Sophia, (28) Simcoe's wife Elizabeth, Royal Navy schooners *Onondaga* (31) and *Mississaga* (32), the Peninsula – now Toronto Island – (33).

VIGNETTE F: A PLACE OF BUSINESS, TOWN OF YORK c.1800
While the first order of business in the newly established community was to provide a measure of defence against the expected attack from south of the border (thus the fortification west of the townsite, now referred to as Fort York), day-to-day commercial activities soon began to fill the town with hustle and bustle.

Woman (34), girl (35), merchant (36), Iroquois woman (37), Iroquois baby (38), still life with contemporary artifacts (39), public notice signed by Executive Council clerk John Small, December 29, 1798 (40).

VIGNETTE G: DAY'S END c.1800
Diarist (41), painting of Jordan's York Hotel (42). The York Hotel, situated on the site of the *Toronto Sun* Building, was Toronto's first.

VIGNETTE H: AN AFFAIR OF HONOUR, JANUARY 3, 1800
In the formative days of our community, John Small (43) and John White (44) were two of the young province's most influential government officials. The former was the clerk of the Executive Council, the latter, the province's attorney general. One evening in the early winter of 1799–1800, Mrs. Small publicly defamed the honour of Mrs. White. The husbands soon got into the fray and before long Small demanded satisfaction on the field of honour according to the customs of the day. A duel was arranged and on January 3, 1800, the two officials met to settle matters in a field behind the Parliament Buildings which in those days was located at the foot of today's Berkeley Street. With the necessary formalities out of the way, the men paced off the required steps, turned and fired. When the smoke had cleared White lay on the ground, mortally wounded. He died of his wound the following day.

VIGNETTE I: THE CAPTURE OF YORK, APRIL 27, 1812
Though Governor Simcoe had left York in 1796 (one year before York became the official provincial capital), his concerns about the small community of some 700 souls

being attacked by American forces came to pass when on the morning of April 27, 1813, less than one year after the outbreak of what has become known as the War of 1812, a squadron of American naval vessels appeared on the horizon. While the ships' guns raked the small town, troops landed near the foot of today's Roncesvalles Avenue, swept eastward, eventually overruling the town's inadequate defences. Within hours, the "stars and stripes" fluttered over the beleaguered little town. York remained occupied by American forces for almost two weeks with the invaders departing on May 8. The conflict, called President Madison's War by some, continued for another twenty months until ended by the Treaty of Ghent signed in that Belgian city on December 24, 1814.

Ojibwa warrior (45 & 49), Mississauga warrior (46), Corporal, Glengarry Light Infantry Fencibles (47), private, 8th King's Regiment (48), private, 16th U.S. Infantry Regiment (50), privates, 15th U.S. Infantry Regiment (51 & 52), musician, U.S. Foot Artillery (53), landing boats carrying American troops (54), 24-gun Corvette *USS President Madison,* American flagship (55), American General Zebulon Pike (discoverer of Pike's Peak in Colorado, 1806) commanded landing forces, lies mortally wounded following the explosion of the garrison's power magazine (56), American officers (57 & 58), broadside announcing Major-General Isaac Brock's capture of Fort Detroit, August 20, 1812 (59).

VIGNETTE J: THE MACKENZIE REBELLION, DECEMBER 1837
Scottish-born William Lyon Mackenzie (62), newspaper editor and politician (Mackenzie had been appointed the newly created City of Toronto's first mayor in 1834) became so upset at the way the so-called "Family Compact," a small group of élite citizens led by Lieutenant-Governor Sir Francis Bond Head (65), Sheriff William Jarvis (66) and the rector of St. James' John Strachan (67) governed the young province of Upper Canada (after 1867, Ontario) that he vowed to overthrow the government, by force if necessary. And that's exactly what he attempted to do in early December 1837. His plans were thwarted, however, when he and his band of rebels (60, 61 and 63), intent on entering the city and seizing government buildings and officials were routed by loyalists (68 & 69) that included a War of 1812 veteran Colonel James Fitzgibbon (64). Mackenzie and many of his followers fled to the United States. Pardoned by Queen Victoria in 1849, he returned to Toronto and moved into a house on Bond Street purchased for him by his admirers. The house, in which "the fiery Scot" died in 1861, is now operated as a museum by the Toronto Historical Board.

VIGNETTE K: THE MARKET, 1835–45
On October 26, 1803, Lieutenant-Governor Peter Hunter proclaimed that henceforth a public market would be held each Saturday on a five-and-a-half-acre site on the south side of King Street near the present Jarvis intersection. At first, market activities took place outdoors or under canvas tents. It wasn't until 1831 that a permanent structure was erected. Then in 1844, the city fathers erected a new City Hall at the southwest corner of Jarvis and Front streets (72 – centre block) at a cost of $52,000. In addition to being the site of municipal government offices, the building also housed shops on

the main floor. The centre portion of this building still stands today, incorporated in the South St. Lawrence market.

In this vignette we see an advertisement of the day (71), man in working clothes of the period (73), an itinerant salesman (74) and a man and woman shopping at the market (75 & 76). Gas lights (70) began lighting Toronto's nights in 1841. Toronto was one of the first cities on the continent to do so.

VIGNETTE L: THE UNDERGROUND RAILWAY, mid-1840s

The *underground railway* was neither underground nor a railway, but a code name for a routing taken by slaves escaping from the intolerable conditions they faced in the American south to safety in the northern states and Canada. Along the way *conductors* assisted the freedom seekers and *stations* were the "safe houses" where protection was provided during the often frightening journey. Toronto was one of many destinations in Ontario for escaping slaves. In this vignette we see escaped slaves (77 & 78) chatting with a sympathizer (79) often referred to as abolitionists.

VIGNETTE M: MEN OF BUSINESS, 1840–50

During this period the population of the city almost doubled from 13,092 in 1840 to more than 25,000 in 1850. Toronto's boundaries were the Don River to the east, Bloor Street to the north and Dufferin Street to the west. Some of these new Torontonians are represented in this mural (80, 81, & 82).

VIGNETTE N: A VISITOR TO TORONTO, 1842

While researching material for his book *American Notes* (which was published one year after *Barnaby Rudge* and one year before *A Christmas Carol*), English novelist Charles Dickens (83) visited Toronto in the spring of 1842 arriving early in the evening of May 7 and departing for Kingston the following day at noon. He described our city as being *full of life and motion, bustle, business and improvement* with the streets *well paved and lighted with gas; the houses large and good; the shops excellent.* He also commented on the city's wood-planked sidewalks, the stone prison (foot of Berkeley Street), a handsome church (St. James'), the court house (northwest corner of King and Church streets) and the new Upper Canada College (then on King Street West near Simcoe).

VIGNETTE O: NEW ARRIVALS in the 1840s

Though the Irish had been migrating to the "New World" for decades, it was as a result of the "Great Famine" of the late 1840s that more than half- million Irish emigrated to British North America many making their way to Toronto. Many were forced to cultivate cabbages as a source of both food and income giving rise to the derisive term *Cabbagetown.* In this vignette we see an Irish immigrant woman (84), her baby and child (85 & 86) and two Irish immigrant men (87 & 88).

VIGNETTE P: INDUSTRY in the 1850s

The first steam railway to operate in the Province of Upper Canada (renamed Ontario following Confederation on July 1, 1867) was the newly incorporated Ontario, Simcoe and Huron Union Railway. It's inaugural train was powered by the locomotive *Toronto*

(90) that chugged out of the city on May 16, 1853 on a two-hour, thirty-mile trip to Machell's Corners (now Aurora). The *Toronto* was constructed at James Good's Foundry located near the northwest corner of Yonge and Queen streets and transferred to the little Front Street station via temporary tracks laid on city thoroughfares. Standing beside the twenty-four-ton locomotive are two railway workers (89 & 91).

VIGNETTE Q: WOMEN OF LEISURE in the 1860s

The Misses Leslie (92 & 93) enjoying a game of croquet. George Leslie owned a sprawling seed and plant nursery out Queen Street east of the city. The community that sprang up nearby became known as Leslieville and the dusty north-south concession road Leslie Street. Also in this vignette is Lady Head (94), wife of Sir Edmund Head, governor-in-chief of the United Canadas from 1854–61.

VIGNETTE R: TORONTO'S QUEEN'S OWN RIFLES, 1866

The Queen's Own Rifles, represented in this vignette by four of their members (95, 96, 97 & 98), originated in 1860 as the 2nd Battalion, Volunteer Militia Rifles of Canada (2nd "Queen's Own Rifles"). Early in the morning of June 1, 1866, men and officers of the "Queen's Own" sailed from Toronto to the Niagara frontier to help defend Canada against an invasion of members of the Fenian Brotherhood, an organization of Irish revolutionaries who believed that the first step in liberating Ireland from the British was to capture the latter's North American possession, Canada. In the military action at Ridgeway (near Fort Erie), nine members of Toronto's Queen's Own Rifles were killed. The battalion's other major battle honours include NORTH-WEST CANADA, 1885; SOUTH AFRICA, 1899–1900; VIMY RIDGE, PURSUIT TO MONS, FRANCE AND FLANDERS, 1915–1918; NORMANDY LANDING, THE RHINELAND, NORTH-WEST EUROPE, 1944–1945.

VIGNETTE S: HORSE-DRAWN TRANSPORTATION in the mid-1800s

Public transportation arrived in Toronto in 1849 when cabinet-maker/undertaker Henry Burt Williams instituted a six-passenger horse-drawn omnibus service from the St. Lawrence Market to the popular Red Lion Inn that was located on the east side of Yonge Street, in the suburban community of Yorkville, just north of the present busy Yonge-Bloor intersection. The omnibus shown in this vignette (99) was restored by the TTC and is typical of the earliest types of horse-drawn vehicles in service on Toronto streets more than a century ago.

VIGNETTE T: EARLY TORONTO TRANSPORTATION in the 1890s

Following Henry Burt Williams's pioneering efforts to provide some form of public transportation for the citizens of Toronto, the Toronto Street Railway Company (TSR) was organized in 1861. This new enterprize laid down rails on Yonge, Queen and King streets and began operating a horse-drawn street railway service; hours of operation – sixteen hours per day in summer, fourteen hours per day in winter, fare – five cents cash (no transfers), maximum speed – 6 mph and when tracks blocked by snow, sleighs to be put in service. Towards the end of the TSR's thirty-year franchise the company had 262 cars, 100 omnibuses, 100 sleighs and 1,356 horses. In 1891, a new company was established that was ordered by the city to commence electrification of the system within one year, the entire system to be completely electrified in three. The city's first electric streetcar went into service on Church Street on August 15, 1892. The last horsecar trotted down McCaul Street on August 31, 1894. The electric streetcar (106) in this vignette represents the type of vehicle introduced in 1897. Unfortunately car #505 was destroyed when flames ripped through the carhouse on King Street East on March 25, 1912. Munro Park (shown on the sign on the front of the car) was a popular turn-of-the-century amusement park at the extreme east end of Queen Street and was accessible via the King streetcar route. The passengers (100 & 101) and crew (conductors – 102 & 103, motormen – 104 & 105) are portrayed in costumes of the 1898 era.

VIGNETTE U: TWO PROMINENT CITY "LANDMARKS," c.1880

Toronto's first house of worship was the little Church of England erected at the northeast corner of King and Church streets (the latter street so-named because of its proximity to this new church) during the period 1803–1807. History records that it was constructed by soldiers from Fort York. Over the years the congregation continued to grow in size necessitating a succession of larger and larger churches each of which was known simply as the "church at York." The name St. James' (after St. James the Apostle) wasn't selected until 1828. It wasn't until the fourth structure was consecrated in 1839 and the Bishop's *cathedra* installed that St. James' Church became St. James' Cathedral. Unfortunately this structure was destroyed by fire in 1849.

When the present cathedral (107) was erected in 1850–53 it didn't look much like today's building lacking as it did the lofty spire that would give the church both its distinctive appearance and mention in early twentieth Century city guidebooks as being, at 324 feet from ground level to weathervane, Toronto's tallest structure. The spire was added in 1874, a peel of nine bells in 1865 (a tenth was added in 1928) and a clock that had taken first prize at the 1873 Vienna Exhibition in 1875. It was purchased by a committee of citizens of all faiths and presented to the Cathedral. It's said that ship captains would seek out the illuminated seven foot, four inch in diameter clock-face as their vessels made for the Port of Toronto.

☙

Born on Toronto Island in 1855, Edward "Ned" Hanlan (108) was destined to become one of Toronto's best known athletes. When Ned was a young man rowing was as popular as hockey and baseball are today. In fact, it could be said that Ned was the Babe Ruth of the rowing world. As an Island resident, Ned spent many hours propelling his sleek scull over the calm waters of Toronto Bay. His matchless rowing skills prompted him to enter rowing competitions held all over the world. His first successes were here in Ontario where in 1874, 1875 and 1876 he won the provincial championship. In the latter year, 1876, Ned also won top honours at the Centennial Regatta in Philadelphia much to the frustration of the majority present since the event was held to commemorate the 100th anniversary of the signing of the American Declaration of Independence. In 1878 Ned became Champion of America, in 1879 Champion of England and in 1880, the year Ned turned twenty-five, Champion of the World. Not only did Hanlan become Canada's first "world" champion, his name became a household word around the world.

In later years Ned Hanlan ran a hotel at Hanlan's Point (the westernmost part of Toronto Island that was actually named in honour of his father who had settled there years earlier). In 1898 he was elected alderman for Ward 4, the constituency in which his beloved Toronto Island was located. Ned Hanlan died in 1908 and is buried in the Necropolis.

VIGNETTE V: A MUCH BELOVED BUILDING

The stately Royal Alexandra Theatre (109) was erected in 1907 at a cost of $750,000 (a huge amount of money in those far-off days) by one of the country's most successful, and youngest, entrepreneurs, twenty-two-year-old Cawthra Mulock. Mulock, who travelled extensively, was determined to put his city "on the map" by erecting one of the best "live-theatre" playhouses on the continent right in his own hometown. The name selected for his new theatre, which was designed by Canadian architect John Lyle, honoured the wife of the then reigning monarch who himself is remembered in the name of another King Street landmark, the King Edward Hotel, erected a few blocks to the east four years before the theatre opened. Cawthra Mulock died of influenza during the "Spanish flu" epidemic that ravaged the world soon after the end of the First World War. He was just 33. In 1962, the future of the Royal Alexandra was bleak. More modern theatres had taken its place as the city's leading showplace and demolition seemed to be lurking in the wings. Fortunately, another Toronto entrepreneur came to the rescue. Shopkeeper "extraordinaire" "Honest Ed" Mirvish purchased the Royal Alexandra for $215,000, pumped hundreds of thousands of dollars into its refurbishment and today the beautiful Royal Alexandra, along with Ed and son David Mirvish's new theatre, the nearby Princess of Wales, is once again one of this city's most admired (and active) buildings.

VIGNETTE W: WINTER IN "THE WARD," 1912

For many years the central and northern sections of old St. John's Ward, that part of downtown Toronto bounded, roughly, by College Street on the north, Yonge Street on the east, Queen Street on the south and University Avenue on the west, was referred to as simply "The Ward". It had gained notoriety in the latter years of the nineteenth Century as "the foreign immigrant receiving area" (as exemplified by the two urchins, 111, & 112, depicted in this mural) and it was here that the vast majority of newcomers to Toronto settled and were confronted with living conditions that wouldn't be tolerated today. A typical dwelling in "The Ward" (110) is depicted here.

VIGNETTE X: TYPICAL OFFICE, 1898

Two male (113 & 114) and one female (115) office workers in the City of Toronto Works Department. On the wall is a painting of the recently vacated provincial Parliament Buildings (116) on the north side of Front Street west of Simcoe Street. This building served a variety of purposes (meetings of the Legislature of Upper Canada, a medical school, a lunatic asylum, military barracks and, finally, meetings of the Ontario Legislature). In 1893, the new Parliament Buildings at Queen's Park opened. The old Front Street buildings were demolished in 1902. Also visible is a bird's-eye view of the city (117) as it appeared in the year depicted in this vignette, 1898. In that year Toronto's population was 186,517, the mayor John Shaw, and the streetcar fare five cents (with motormen earning fifteen cents per hour).

VIGNETTE Y: NEW IMMIGRANTS, 1900–1912

Young British immigrants Frank and Arthur Cain (118 & 119) arriving in Toronto. Other immigrants from the British Isles whose names are now well-known in our city's history include the province's first Lieutenant- Governor John Graves Simcoe, his wife Elizabeth, a talented artist and diarist, shopkeepers Timothy Eaton and Robert Simpson, industrialist Hart Massey (Massey Hall and Hart House) and the co-discoverers of insulin, Frederick Banting and Charles Best.

VIGNETTE Z: TORONTO BEFORE THE FIRST WORLD WAR, 1908–1913

Soaring into the heavens at the southeast corner of Yonge and King streets the Canadian Pacific Railway Building (120) was for a time "the tallest structure in the British Empire" wrestling that description after its opening in 1913 from its slightly less lofty neighbour next door, a structure that was originally the head office of the long-defunct Traders Bank. Both historic skyscrapers still stand, virtually hidden amongst Toronto's modern-day skyscrapers. The main floor of the CPR Building, now occupied by a drug mart, originally housed busy ticketing offices where passengers could obtain passage on the hundreds of trains leaving Toronto destined for innumerable cross-Canada destinations.

One of the most prominent civic politicians of the pre-war era was William Peyton Hubbard (121). His contributions to Toronto are best summarized on an historic plaque erected in 1979 near his Broadview Avenue residence by the Toronto Historical Board that reads:

William Peyton Hubbard (1842–1935)

660 Broadview Avenue was the home of William Hubbard, Toronto's first black politician. The Toronto-born son of a freed slave from Virginia, Hubbard was elected to City Council in 1894 and served for a total of fifteen years, frequently as Senior Controller. He was a champion of the rights of various minorities and pioneer in the founding of Toronto Hydro. Hubbard also served in such capacities as justice of the peace, school trustee, Toronto Harbour commissioner and, for four decades, as a representative to the House of Industry.

In pre-war Toronto, the Canadian National Exhibition was truly "the showplace of the Nation" where "firsts" in the fields of transportation, communication, home appliances, etc. were introduced to the Canadian public as represented by the two gentlemen (122 & 123) inspecting a new auto in this vignette. The "Ex" originated in 1879 as the Toronto Industrial Exhibition.

VIGNETTE AA: THE GREAT WAR

The ink on Canada's declaration of war against Germany was barely dry when the first Torontonians began "signing up." One of the first groups to head overseas was the 3rd Canadian Battalion Toronto Regiment (represented in this vignette by 125, 126 & 127) made up mainly of men and officers of the Queen's Own Rifles, Toronto's oldest regiment with origins dating back to 1860. Of the 626,636 Canadians who fought in the "war to end all wars" more than 66,000 were from Toronto. Of that number, 10,000 made the supreme sacrifice.

The war was just weeks old when the Directors of the Canadian National Exhibition offered Exhibition Park and its numerous permanent buildings to the military to be used as a barracks for as long as the war lasted. During the summer months officers and men assigned to Camp CNE were under canvas at Niagara-on-the-Lake permitting the annual fair to be held where visitors (128 & 129) were given a glimpse of military life.

The backdrop in the vignette (124) features aircraft insignia and colour schemes that became familiar to members of the Royal Flying Corps (RFC) many of whom were Toronto boys. One of the RFC's most important training schools was the Armour Heights airfield located north of the city on a site now occupied by the present busy Highway 401/Avenue Road intersection.

VIGNETTE BB: BETWEEN THE WARS, 1920–32

With the end of the war, one of the most notable changes on the streets of Toronto was the vastly increased number of private automobiles. One of the most popular makes was the Oshawa-built McLaughlin with a 1921 Master Six Roadster model seen here (130). Three years earlier McLaughlin and Chevrolet amalgamated to form General Motors of Canada. The McLaughlin nameplate (renamed McLaughlin-Buick) vanished in 1942.

Often referred to as the world's first true movie "star" Mary Pickford (131) was born in 1893 in a small two-storey house on a then residential University Avenue (a site now occupied by a portion of the world-famous Hospital for Sick Children). The eldest child of John and Charlotte Smith, Gladys Marie changed her name on the advice of legendary Broadway producer David Belasco – Mary from Marie and Pickford from her maternal grandfather John Pickford Hennessey. For twenty-three years Mary was the undisputed "Queen of the silent screen" starring in 125 short features and fifty-two full-length films. Her first film appearance was in *The Violin Maker of Cremona* (1909); her last in *Secrets* (1933). Mary Pickford died in 1979.

In the depths of the Great Depression the Canadian National Exhibition continued to provide visitors with a glimmer of hope and a source of amusement. The traditional Grandstand Spectacular at the 1932 Ex (as advertised on that year's colourful poster, 132) was titled *The Triumph*.

The Toronto Maple Leaf hockey team was born in February 1927 following the acquisition of the old Toronto St. Pats team by Connie Smythe who renamed the team in recognition of the maple leaf badge he wore on his uniform while overseas in the First World War. In 1932, Maple Leaf hockey stars Charlie Conacher (133), Harvey "Busher" Jackson (134) and Joe Primeau (135) helped the team win its first Stanley Cup (136). Leafs beat the New York Rangers three games to none in a best-of-five final. The Leafs moved from the old Arena on Mutual Street to the new Maple Leaf Gardens on November 12, 1931.

Albert Franck (1899–1977) came to Canada from his native Holland in 1926 and while working as a picture restorer in a small shop on Gerrard Street near Bay, a neighbourhood regarded as Toronto's version of New York City's famous Greenwich Village, began painting his impressions of Toronto street scenes, backyards and houses. Over the years Franck's numerous works, one of which *Behind Robert Street* painted in 1967 is depicted here (137), have become eagerly sought after by collectors.

Authorized as the Royal Canadian Air Force's No. 10 (Army Co-operation) Squadron Auxiliary on October 5, 1932, this pioneer flying corps became affiliated with the City of Toronto in 1935 and officially renumbered and renamed No. 110 "City of Toronto" Squadron (Auxiliary) in late 1937. At this time the squadron had a total of four de Havilland DH-60 *Gypsy Moths*, similar to #158 seen in this vignette (138) and operated out of the historic de Lesseps Air Field (where the first airplane to fly over Toronto took off and landed in 1910) in suburban Weston. Soon after the outbreak of the Second World War, the squadron was sent to Odiham, Hampshire, England and on March 1, 1941, renumbered No. 400 Squadron. Throughout the war the unit flew photographic reconnaissance using a variety of aircraft, Lysanders, Tomahawks, Mosquitos and Spitfires. A total of twenty-eight No. 400 personnel were killed during the war. The squadron was disbanded in the summer of 1945 only to be reactivated as No. 400 "City of Toronto" Squadron (Auxiliary) less than a year later. In its capacity as an Air Defence unit, No. 400 pilots flew Vampires, T-33s and Sabres. In 1958, the squadron was reassigned to Air Transport Command and the jets were replaced by Expeditors and Otters. The squadron is presently (1994) an Air Reserve Helicopter Operational Training Squadron and flies Bell CH-136 Kiowas.

Professional baseball has been a popular summer pastime in Toronto for more than a century with the earliest games played in stadiums near the mouth of the Don River, over at Toronto Island and in later years at the foot of Bathurst Street. On April 7, 1977, the newly franchised Blue Jays of the American League began playing at Exhibition Stadium (defeating Chicago 9 to 5) moving to SkyDome (where they lost to Milwaukee 5 to 3) on June 5, 1989. One of the most popular players on the Maple Leaf teams of yesteryear was Luke "Hot Potato" Hamlin (139) who during his years with Toronto (1933–48) pitched a total of 149 games winning a highly respectable 91.

The artist's father, Hugh Hood, (140) and Hugh's best friend, Ronnie Biggar (141), in 1946.

Without question, the *CF-105 Arrow* (142) was the most controversial aircraft to ever fly in this country. Designed and built by A.V. Roe Canada Ltd. at its Malton, Ontario, plant (adjacent to Malton, now Pearson International Airport), this highly advanced, delta-wing supersonic jet interceptor first flew on March 25, 1958, number 201 depicted here having that honour. The *Arrow's* flying characteristics quickly exceeded those of any aircraft flying anywhere in the world. In total only five were completed and test flown before the entire program was canceled by the government on February 20, 1959. Citing high costs and imminent obsolescence of manned jet fighters, all five *Arrows* were summarily cut into pieces and all relevant documents and highly specialized fabrication machinery destroyed. Many of the engineers and technicians who worked on the *Arrow* project were subsequently employed by the National Aeronautics and Space Administration (NASA) where they were instrumental in getting the first men to the moon.

As a feature of the 1954 edition of the Canadian National Exhibition, the directors had arranged that internationally famous American swimming star Florence Chadwick would attempt to become the first person in history to swim across Lake Ontario. If successful in completing the treacherous 51.5 kilometres (32 miles) from Youngstown, New York, to the CNE waterfront Florence would be awarded the astronomical sum (for the day) of $10,000. It came as a surprise to everyone that when Chadwick was pulled from the icy water only twenty-six kilometres (sixteen miles) from the starting point, sixteen-year-old Toronto schoolgirl Marilyn Bell (143), an unofficial entrant who was "swimming for Canada" and had plunged into the lake just minutes after Chadwick, was still going strong. After twenty hours and fifty-seven minutes a dazed and weary Marilyn touched the breakwall south of the Boulevard Club at 8:04 PM. September 9, 1954, to become the first person in history to swim Lake Ontario. The following year Marilyn became the youngest person to conquer the English Channel and in 1956 she swam the formidable Strait of Juan de Fuca between the state of Washington and British Columbia. Marilyn, now Marilyn Di Lascio, retired teacher and mother of four, presently lives with her husband, Joe, in New Jersey.

VIGNETTE DD: TORONTO ARTS AND CULTURE FROM POST WAR TO CONTEMPORARY

(144) Toronto-born pianist Glenn Gould (1932–1982).

(145) Toronto-born actor Walter Huston (1884–1950) as he appeared in the 1948 film classic *The Treasure of the Sierra Madre,* a role that earned him an Academy Award for "Best Supporting Actor."

(146) London, England-born actress Kate Reid (1930–93) was educated at the University of Toronto. She appeared on stage, screen and television in both Canada and the United States.

(147) Ottawa-born poet and novelist Margaret Atwood (1939–) is a graduate of the University of Toronto.

(148) Toronto-born painter and printmaker Harold Town (1924–1990).

(149) Alberta-born comunications theorist Marshall "The Medium is the Message" McLuhan (1911–80) was educated at the University of Alberta and Cambridge and taught at the University of Toronto's St. Michael's College establishing U of T's "Centre for Culture and Technology" in 1963.

(150) Actor Graham Greene (1953–) was born on the Six Nations reserve near Brantford, Ontario.

(151) Alberta-born actress Tantoo Cardinal (1950–).

(152) Manitoba-born playwrite Tomson Highway (1951–).

(153) Painting by Harold Town completed in 1963 titled *Imaginary Portrait of William Kilbourn as a Young Poet.*

(154) Painting by Toronto-born Joyce Wieland *Time Machine Series* done in 1961.

(155) Painting of Hart House. Given to the University of Toronto by the Massey Foundation and providing athletic, social and dining facilities for university students, Hart House was planned by Vincent Massey as a memorial to his father, Hart Massey. The structure was built over the period 1911–19. Soldier's Tower was dedicated in 1924 to the memory of students who died in the First World War.

VIGNETTE EE: THE SUN FOUNDERS

Douglas Creighton (156), Donald Hunt (157), Edward Dunlop (158) and Peter Worthington (159).

VIGNETTE FF: TORONTO RECENTLY 1992 to the present

Toronto Island ferryboat *Sam McBride* (160) approaching Centre Island dock. Ferries of all shapes and sizes have transported visitors to Toronto Island since 1833 when the first, a two-horsepower vessel (utilizing the power of two horses walking a circular treadmill connected by gears to sidepaddles), entered service. The double-end, propeller-driven diesel *Sam McBride* entered service in 1939 and is named for Mayor McBride who died while in office. Others in the present-day fleet (and year they entered service) include *William Inglis* (1935), *Thomas Rennie* (1950), *Ongiara* (1963) and *Trillium*, the pride of the fleet. Entering service in 1910, this steam-powered side-paddle vessel was restored in 1973–76.

Toronto City Hall (161), designed by Finnish architect Viljo Revell and the winner of a world-wide competition, was built during the period 1961–65.

Cityscape (162) featuring the CN Tower (at 1,815 feet, 5 inches/553 meters, the tallest free-standing structure in the world) and SkyDome with its fully retractable roof in the closed position. The three-moveable, one-fixed panel roof takes 20 minutes to open or close. The CN Tower was officially opened on June 26, 1976; SkyDome on June 3, 1989.

Participants (163, 164, 165 & 166) in the 1992 edition of the Caribana festival.

Toronto Blue Jays' second baseman Roberto Alomar (167) and right fielder Joe Carter (168) celebrating 1992 World Series victory. The Jays entered the American League in 1977 playing team home games at Exhibition Stadium. In 1989 they moved to the new SkyDome where, on October 24, 1992, they defeated the Atlanta Braves 4 games to 2 to become the first non-U.S. team to win the World Series title. The Blue Jays retained the title in 1993.

Toronto Maple Leaf's Doug Gilmour (169) and Los Angeles King's Wayne Gretzky (170) confront each other during an NHL conference final at Maple Leaf Gardens, 1993.

Toronto Blue Jay first baseman John Olerud (171) sets new club record by hitting in twenty-three consecutive games. The record was set on June 18, 1993 when he hit a double off Boston Red Sox pitcher Roger Clemens in an 11 to 2 Jays victory.

Nanny and baby (172 & 173), baby holding Barney the Dinosaur (174).

Man, woman and baby (175, 176 & 177) strolling along Front Street East in the summer of 1993. This trio captured the eye of artist Hood and are now immortalized in his mural.

Paul Godfrey, president and chief executive officer of the *Toronto Sun* and champion of this mural (178).

Jean Stilwell (179) as Carmen in the 1993 Canadian Opera Company production of Georges Bizet's masterpiece.

Metro Toronto police constable (180) on community patrol, 1993.

Toronto Transit Commission streetcar (181) on the 504 King route, 1993. Toronto has been a "streetcar city" since the first horsecars entered service in 1861. The system was electrified in 1892–94. The streetcar depicted in the mural is a Canadian Light Rail Vehicle, the first of which entered service in 1979. CLRVs were first seen on the 504 King line on July 20, 1981. While the westbound 504 King destination is usually Dundas West Station, on the days the artist painted CLRV 4083, all 504 King cars were being "short turned" at Dufferin due to a major track rehabilitation job on King Street west of Dufferin.

Young boy and girl (182, 183) watching John work on his mural.

Trio of Metro Toronto Works Department employees (184, 185 and 186), hard at work on Front Street east in the summer of 1993.

John Hood

Detail of Avro *Arrow* (#142 in guide)

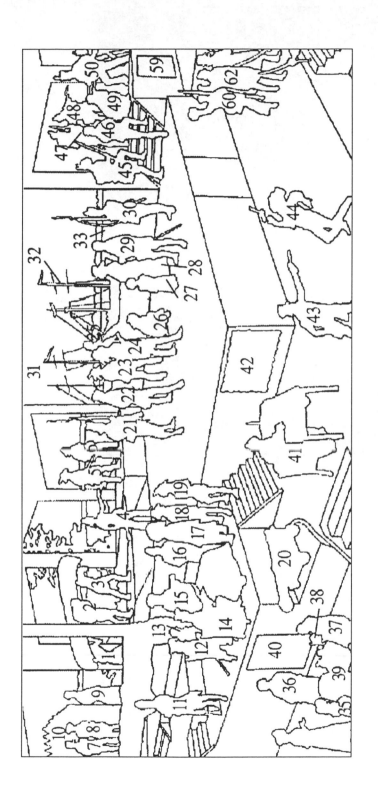

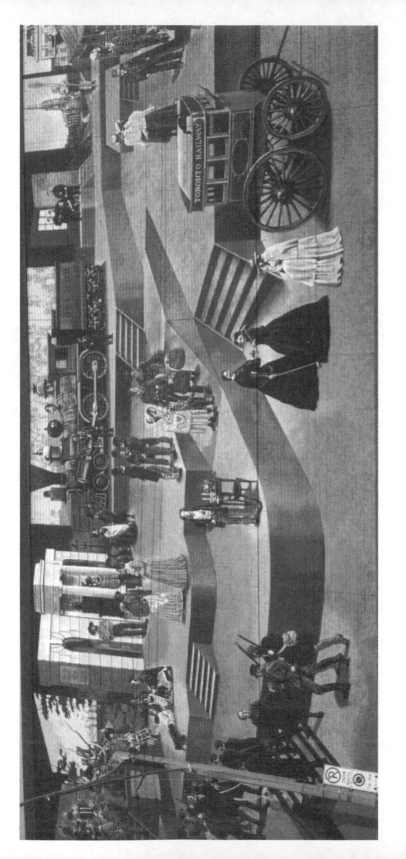

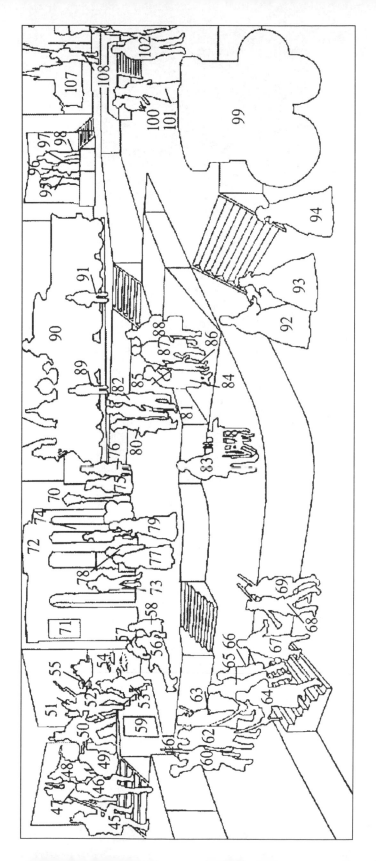

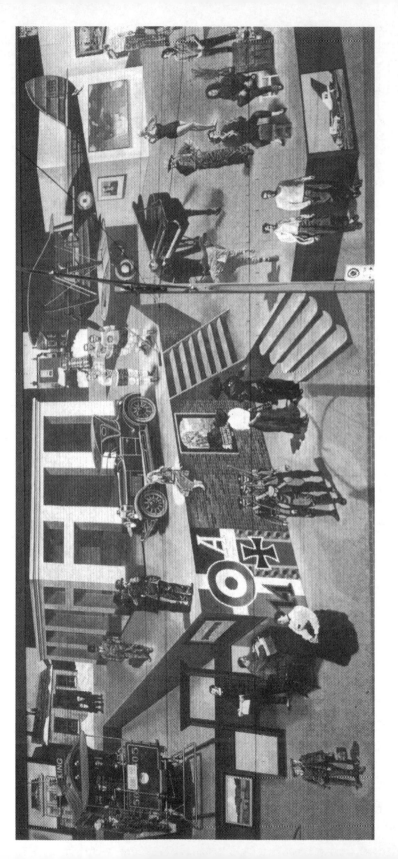

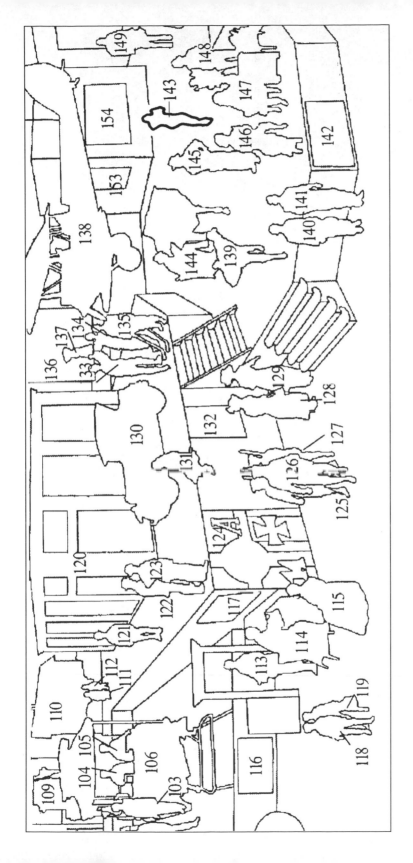

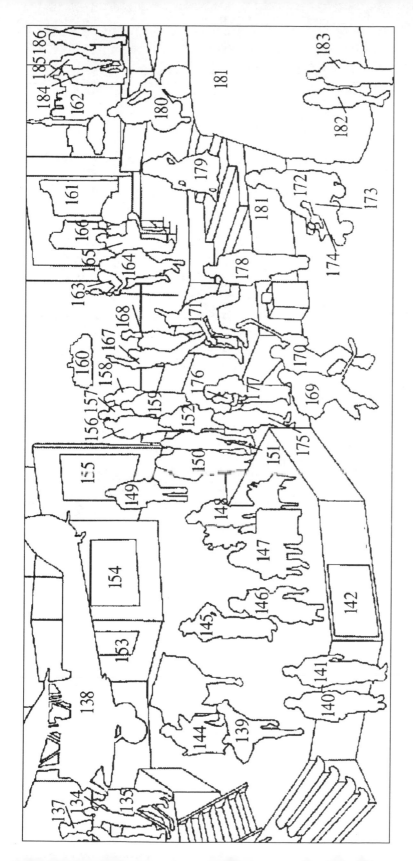

TALKIN' TRASH

September 12, 1993

This week's column is garbage or, to be more precise, about garbage. With the traffic restrictions in place at the south end of the Don Valley Parkway, morning rush hour drivers now have a great opportunity to get a closer look at the hulking brick building with soaring chimney located to the east of the Parkway just south of the Gerrard Street bridge.

The new Don Destructor on the east bank of the river just north of Dundas Street shortly after it opened in 1917. *(CTA)*

In 1917, this large destructor (a term that has since been replaced by the word incinerator) was an important feature in coming to grips with the city's growing garbage disposal problem.

The city had actually entered the incineration business many years before when in 1890 a rudimentary facility opened on Eastern Avenue near the Don River. Over the succeeding years more modern plants were erected including one adjacent to the Don River, and others on Commissioners Street,

The abandoned destructor as it looks today.

Wellington Street West and Symes Road. As recently as 1965, more than 80 percent, or 1,400 tons of the city's daily 1,700 ton garbage load, was being burned.

The Don Incinerator closed in 1970 with all incineration of garbage ending just a few years ago with the closing of the Commissioners Street plant.

The earliest references to the disposal of garbage in York (as our city was known until 1834 when city status was achieved and the name changed back to the original Toronto) was pretty much limited to dumping what little garbage there was into a hole and covering it with dirt or, in the winter months, simply placing garbage (including various dead animals) on the ice that covered the

Toronto Bay and waiting until the warmer spring weather caused the problem to literally disappear from view.

As the years went by, the ongoing filling in of the harbour to create new land provided another perfect place to dump for unwanted materials. In fact, during excavations for SkyDome workers would frequently come across accumulations of waste materials including a batch of empty bottles, one of which, was estimated to be more than 100 years old, and still contained traces and the odour of mustard.

Another depository for waste materials was Ashbridge's Bay, in its original state simply a collection of small ponds and narrow fingers of land. Its reclamation in the early years of this century, through the dumping of a variety of materials, has resulted in the land mass at the east end of the harbour.

Another site was behind the sea wall at the Exhibition on which the present Lake Shore Boulevard was eventually laid out.

Other areas used for the disposal of street sweepings, household garbage and ashes (there's something no one puts out at the curb any more) included valleys and other low areas where material could be dumped to bring the depressions up to grade and on which parks and streets would frequently emerge.

The newspapers of the day made specific references to landfill sites on Pendrith Avenue, the Harrison Street "extension," and at the corner of Bloor Street and Woodville Avenue, the latter thoroughfare renamed Indian Grove in the teens. As late as 1965, refuse was still being used as landfill on Pottery Road just east of the Bayview Extension.

In late 1911, as the refuse problem continued to worsen, the city was presented with an extensive report that recommended that Toronto separate its garbage load into its three major components: garbage, which would be treated in a massive reduction facility, rubbish, taken to incinerators and burned, and ashes that would be used as landfill as needed.

The latter two methods are self-explanatory and, as already stated, extensively used by the city.

The first method, reduction, involved dumping the garbage in huge digesters and cooking the mass under steam pressure for several hours. The liquid would then be drawn off into large separator tanks where the grease, which would collect on the surface, would be collected and sold for use in various products such as soaps. The remaining liquid would be treated in the sewage treatment system.

The solid mass that's left would be pressed, to remove as much liquid as possible, dried and marketed as well, its residual components being valuable in the manufacture of fertilizers.

The reduction process did have one drawback. Most gave off terrible odours. For this and other reasons, city officials never acted on the report. As a result, incineration and landfilling methods continued.

Today, with incineration prohibited and landfill sites about to overflow, the disposal of garbage remains a topic of concern.

BRAVE NEW "T.O."

September 12, 1993

This article was written in honour of the Sunday Sun's *twentieth anniversary and appeared in addition to my regular "The Way We Were" column.*

While I can't claim to be a "day-oner" with the *Sunday Sun*, I do take some pride in the fact that my *"The Way We Were"* column became a component of the paper just months after the premier edition rolled off the presses on September 16, 1973.

Now, for someone who writes about the "good old days," say fifty, sixty, seventy years, or even longer ago than that, the idea of writing about things that happened a mere twenty years ago didn't really seem that interesting. After all, twenty years ago ... that was just the other day.

After spending a few hours perusing the newspapers of the day, then some more time looking through a few reference books it became apparent that 1973 was a busy year though many of its stories have become simply vague happenings on history's blackboard.

With the United States involvement in the Vietman crisis drawing to a close following a January 28 ceasefire, the most important story to continue percolating throughout 1973 was the ever-deepening Watergate Hotel fiasco culminating late in the year with the release of a few of the now famous Oval Office tape recordings complete with some very suspect gaps in many of President Nixon's conversations.

It was also in 1973 that the Bahamas finally gained full independence from Great Britain. It was also the year that the fourth and fiercest Arab-Israeli War since 1948 erupted. By the end of the year the world was in the grips of a severe energy crisis that would soon lead to lengthy lineups at gas station pumps, curtailment of numerous airline flights and soaring consumer costs virtually across the board.

In American grocery stores, packages imprinted with something called the Universal Product Code began to appear on shelves. Promoters of the new technology hoped that by electronically scanning the little black lines of varying widths that made up the UPC both checkout and inventory control would become easier. Many customers, however, spent 1973 protesting the removal of individually marked prices.

On a less dismal note, 1973 was the year that Mrs. Billie Jean King defeated former Wimbledon champion Bobby Riggs in a tennis match billed as "the battle of the sexes," It was also the year that American Baseball League introduced the "designated hitter" rule with one of their member teams, the

Oakland A's, defeating the New York Mets 4 games to 3 to secure that year's edition of the World Series. And while the 1973–74 NHL hockey season was still a few weeks away from opening when the *Sunday Sun* made its initial appearance on September 16, the Montreal Canadiens under Scotty Bowman were the reigning 1972–73 Stanley Cup champions, an honour they'd relinquish the following season to the Flyers from Philadelphia. And a few weeks after the *Sunday Sun* first appeared, Ottawa defeated Edmonton 22 to 18 to win the 1973 Grey Cup.

The most frequently heard songs eminating from radios, cassette players and 8-track tape decks the day the *Sunday Sun* first rolled off the presses were *Delta Dawn* by Helen Reddy, *Say, Has Anybody Seen My Sweet Gypsy Rose* by Tony Orlando and Dawn, and Marvin Gaye's *Let's Get It On.*

Big at Toronto theatres that same day were *The Sound of Music* at the Eglinton, *Jesus Christ, Superstar* at the University, *Last Tango in Paris* at the Towne Cinema and *Sleuth* at the Glendale. And while all of these films have survived on video cassettes, only the Eglinton Theatre is still with us. Oh, by the way, should you plan to take the TTC, the adult fare is still 30¢, but there's talk they'll have to raise it soon.

After the show, you might want to visit one of the city's popular dining spots like the Savarin on Bay Street, the Friar's over on Yonge, the Towne and Country on Mutual or the elegant Franz Joseph Room in the Walker House Hotel. They're all gone too.

Here in Canada, 1973 saw Pierre Trudeau in the driver's seat up in Ottawa, while in Ontario Bill Davis was still in the early stages of what would become a lengthy fourteen-year tenure.

Locally, results of the December 1972 municipal election confirmed that former Ward 11 alderman David Crombie would serve as mayor of Toronto for 1973–74. He would ultimately serve as the city's chief magistrate until mid-1978 when he resigned to seek a federal seat.

As popular as "the tiny perfect" fellow was, his forty-five-foot holding bylaw created a great deal of consternation and general gnashing of teeth throughout the community's real estate development industry as Crombie and his council fought to retain control over the destiny of "the city of neighborhoods."

One member serving on Crombie's powerful Executive Committee during this, one of the most important periods in the city's history, was hard working Ward 4 alderman Art Eggelton who would stick around after Crombie went to Ottawa. Art would eventually become mayor himself and serve a record-breaking eleven years before he, too, would head off for Parliament Hill.

Other area municipality mayors to serve on the Metro Toronto Council twenty years ago were Paul Cosgrove (Scarborough), Willis Blair (East York), Dennis Flynn (Etobicoke), Melvin (that's the way it appears in the official records) Lastman (North York) and Philip White (York).

In appearance, the Toronto of 1973 was quite different than the Toronto of today. A list of structures that we didn't have back then would include the Harbour Castle Hilton (now Westin) on the water's edge, the Eaton Centre, Roy Thomson Hall, the Metro Library, the Sun Life Centre, Scotia Plaza, SkyDome and BCE Place, all of which were still a few years in the city's future.

Nonetheless, in 1973 we had a nice collection of skyscrapers to admire and show-off to visitors. Structures like the T-D Centre (completed in 1971) and Commerce Court (1972) with a pair of old landmarks, the Bank of Commerce Building and Royal York Hotel, still quite prominent on the skyline. And if you looked closely you

Two Toronto landmarks, one old, the other brand new, as they appeared in 1973, the year the *Sunday Sun* was first published. In the photo the 1910 Toronto Island ferry *Trillium* awaits a restoration while the familiar outline of the new CN Tower, without its Sky Pod, Space Deck or sky scratching antenna, starts to take shape.

could still make out the 300-foot-high clock tower of "old" (1899) City Hall and next to it, the distinctive 1965 City Hall of Viljo Revell.

As the year 1973 evolved (and plans to publish a Sunday edition of the *Sun* were being formulated), a couple of new buildings began to take shape to once again alter the city's constantly changing skyline. At the northwest corner of King and Bay streets, construction of the new seventy-two-storey First Canadian Place was underway (it would be completed in 1975 and remains as the country's tallest building) while just down the street, the gorgeous Royal Bank Plaza, destined to mimic a huge chadelier of golden glass, was being assembled.

The indisputable champion of construction projects underway the year the *Sunday Sun* first appeared was our very own CN Tower. Though months had been spent on site preparation, actual construction of the world's tallest free standing structure began in early 1973. By the end of the year the tower was teasing viewers with just a hint of what it would look like upon completion, a look that would quickly become a symbol of Toronto to the entire world.

GETTING FILL OF
GARBAGE PROBLEMS

September 19, 1993

In last week's column I touched upon the city's early attempts to come to grips with its constantly worsening garbage disposal problem. Starting with the simple landfilling approach, then to a period of time during which incineration seemed to be the ultimate answer, we've once again reverted to landfilling as the remedy to the garbage problem plaguing our modern society.

Sure, there's a greater emphasis on reuse and recycling, but sticking tons of garbage into large holes in the ground is today's easy answer.

That's not to say that efforts weren't made to help alleviate the problem. As noted last week, a 1911 plan would have seen a large portion of the city's garbage (not to be confused with either the more innocuous rubbish or plain ordinary street sweepings) treated with heat and steam and converted into marketable by-products.

Foot of Spadina Avenue (Spadina bridge, demolished, in background, Steele-Briggs Seed building, still standing, at top right, Loretto Abbey, demolished, at top left). *(CTA)*

Several years before that, and, as it happens, ninety years ago this year, a news item in the October 14, 1903 edition of the *Evening Telegram* revealed that at the city's Works Committee meeting held that day the value of removing street sweepings to the Island where the material would be mixed

South of new Toronto Harbour Commission building.
(THC)

with the soil was discussed. It was agreed that natural mineral content of the sweepings would act as good fertilizer.

Also before the committee was Edward Tyrell who wished permission to erect a garbage reduction plant where organic material would be turned into a saleable tea-like substance.

In both cases, the ideas were held for further discussion. Nothing appears to have happened. While its true that the Island has doubled in area (360 acres in 1912 to 820 acres today) most of this was done through the depositing of material from the bottom of Toronto Bay during harbour dredging operations.

Of particular interest in the ninety-year-old news item is a statement that many of the city's existing dump sites were rapidly filling up. They were: one and a half miles along Cherry Street, one and a third miles along Park Road, the Don flats opposite Winchester Street, foot of Caroline Street, west side of Ossington north of Churchill Street, ravine at Bloor and Clinton streets, ravine on Garden Avenue, Bedford Road and Exhibition Park.

Alderman Burns suggested depositing garbage along the city's waterfront from Bathurst Street to Sunnyside to a width of 100 yards. It was his plan to have a boulevard drive constructed on top of the garbage, a thoroughfare that would become "one of the most beautiful drives imaginable." Lake Shore Boulevard opened in the 1920s.

Accompanying this article are photos of other Toronto "garbage disposal" sites in the 1920s.

BASEBALL FEVER

October 10, 1993

Once again Toronto is in the grips of baseball fever as our Blue Jays strive for their second consecutive World Series crown.

For many younger Torontonians, and for many newcomers to our city, this passion for baseball, especially at this time of the year, would seem to be a new phenomenon. Actually, fall baseball championship fever is an affliction that first befell citizens of this city more than a century ago.

That's not to say that the game itself has only been enjoyed by Toronto fans since the waning years of the last century. In fact, baseball made an appearance in Toronto many years earlier as described in a newspaper account of 1859; "A number of young men of this city have organized

Toronto, 1913

While Toronto's professional baseball team attracted thousands to the stadium at Hanlan's Point, numerous other amateur teams such as the Wychwood B.B.C., 1913 Senior Champions, posing for a team portrait in the accompanying photo, provided entertainment at ball parks on the mainland.
The photo was provided by reader Alldyn Clark who asks if anyone knows anything further about the Wychwood team. If you do please drop me note and I'll pass the details on.
Still waiting for an answer.

themselves into a baseball club called the *Canadian Pioneers*. They practice every Monday afternoon at 4 p.m. on the University grounds."

The game remained a novelty for the next few years taking a back seat to the much more popular lacrosse then regarded as the country's national sport.

An attempt was made in 1876 (the same year that the first true professional association, the present National League, was established) to convert baseball from a kind of obscure "after work diversion" into a professional event when a local team called the Clippers entered the new Canadian Professional Baseball League playing teams from London, Guelph, Port Hope, Markham and Kingston. That term "professional" really only meant that the winner of each match would receive a prize of ten dollars, so in the truest sense these fellows were playing not just for fun, as had been the custom, but were actually playing for money.

It seemed that not all Ontarians were ready to embrace pro baseball and the country's first professional league folded after just one season.

Nevertheless, the teams from London and Guelph went on to join a new International Association in which teams from both sides of the border did battle. Most baseball historians agree that this was the sport's first minor league. To add insult to injury, London surprised the American competitors when, in 1877, they won the league title.

Over the next few years baseball, though certainly not as popular as lacrosse and cricket, gained more and more supporters. By the mid-1880s, local businessmen, sensing there was money to be made in organized baseball, began agitating for a team that would represent Toronto. Following a meeting in the Rossin House Hotel (later the Prince George and a site now occupied by structures at the west end of the T-D Centre), it was decided that 500 shares in a new baseball club would be sold at ten dollars a share, the Jarvis Lacrosse Field (northwest corner of Jarvis and Wellesley streets) would become home ground, a manager from south of the border would be hired and, finally, no more than four players from Toronto would be allowed on the roster.

The team's first two games were less than memorable with the *Torontos* losing both. On June 15, 1885, the third match and the team's first home game was different, the local "ball tossers" defeating the Guelph Maple Leafs 8 to 5. At season's end, the Toronto team ranked third winning twenty-four of its forty-four games. Financially, the experiment was a success with gate receipts totaling $8,500 and players' salaries amounting to $4,231. Professional baseball had experienced a successful inaugural year in Toronto and it wasn't long before some people began pushing for the team to seek entry into the majors.

While acceptance into the American League wouldn't come for another nine decades, Toronto did become a founding member of the new International League in which the team continued to play (except for the five-year period 1891–95) from 1886 until fan disinterest and subsequent bankruptcy terminated local professional baseball in 1967. In an attempt to defend the Toronto team's apparent defection to the new league, a Hamilton newspaper editorialized in a February 24, 1886 column that "professional baseball is a pure matter of business. Large salaries are paid to the players and heavy expenses are incurred in the management of the teams." Prophetic words indeed.

During its seventy-six-year term as a member of the International League, Toronto home fields were located near the mouth of the Don River (Toronto Baseball Grounds, later Sunlight Park), at Toronto Island (Hanlan's Point Stadium, later rebuilt and renamed Maple Leaf Stadium), north of the CNE grounds (Diamond Park), and at the foot of Bathurst Street (another Maple Leaf Stadium).

Then came the Blue Jays and after only fifteen seasons Toronto became home to the World Series champions. And this year ...

After becoming the first Canadian team to win the World Series in 1992, the Jays repeated their success in 1993. No World Series championship was held in 1994, so the Blue Jays remain the champions.

GETTYSBURG CARNAGE

October 17, 1993

I went to see the new film *Gettysburg* the other evening and enjoyed all 250 plus minutes of it. And while the battle fought at that small Pennsylvania town, a battle that history would later define as the turning point in the American Civil War, would, at first glance, appear to have involved only citizens of the American Confederate and Union states, countless numbers of Canadians were also participants, and victims.

I use the term countless because while regimental histories reveal that tens of thousands of citizens of British North America signed up to fight on both the Union and Confederate sides, no one has yet resolved just how many of that number died during the three-days of carnage that drenched the rolling wheat fields around that small Pennsylvanian town with the blood of more than 51,000 victims.

Our country's part in the Civil War stemmed from rather simple

Toronto-born William McDougall (1822–1905), a "Father of Canadian Confederation," was present at the dedication of the Soldier's Cemetery when President Lincoln gave his now famous Gettysburg Address.

beliefs of many of its citizens, some of whom fought on the side of the Union as a way of demonstrating their opposition to the practice of slavery. Others, fearing an all-out attack on their homeland by victorious Union troops, joined with the Confederate forces to defeat "Billy Yank."

Some reference works suggest that as many as 50,000 Canadians were participants in the bloody four-year struggle that resulted in the death of more than 600,000 brave men. There's little doubt that the confederation of our nation's original four provinces into a country called Canada was hastened thanks to concerns that arose during the American Civil War.

On a cold November morning, less than five months after the carnage at Gettysburg, a speech was given by a grieving president. That speech, which concludes "... that we here highly resolve that these dead shall not have died in vain; that this nation, under God, shall have a new birth of freedom, and that this government of the people, by the people, and for the people shall not per-ish from the earth" was given by President Abraham Lincoln at the November 19, 1863 dedication ceremony of what we now know as the Gettysburg National Cemetery where the remains of 3,512 Union soldiers have been interred.

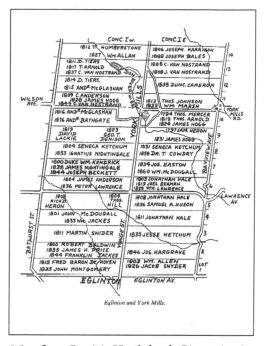

Eglinton and York Mills.

(At the time, hostilities towards the south still ran high and the Confederate dead were left on the battlefield in vast mass graves. In 1872, these bodies were removed and reinterred in cemeteries in the southern cities of Richmond, Charleston, Savannah and Raleigh.)

Present at that consecration ceremony was a young Torontonian and member of the Parliament of United Canada (as the federation of Ontario and Quebec was known from 1841 to 1867).

William McDougall (whose fascinating story was docu-

Map from Patricia Hart's book *Pioneering in North York* (General Publishing, 1968) showing McDougall's property northeast of the modern Yonge Street/Lawrence Avenue intersection.

mented in the June 18, 1925 edition of the Toronto *Evening Telegram)* was born in 1822 (when Toronto was stilled called York) and while still a youngster moved, with his parents, to Grandfather McDougall's farm, lot 4, 1st concession west, York Township (on a modern map, it would have been situated on the west side of Yonge, just south of Lawrence Avenue). In later years he would acquire property a little further north, lot 7, 1st concession east (Bowood Avenue, east of Yonge). Here, just west of where the Don River flows under the modern Bayview bridge north of Lawrence, he operated a lumber mill.

McDougall was educated at Victoria College, then still in Cobourg, and entered politics in 1858 as a member for North Oxford. Over the years, his diplomatic reputation became well known and in November of 1863 was dispatched on a mission to Washington, D.C. In a brief meeting with President Lincoln on the 17th, McDougall was advised that the conference scheduled for the following day would have to be postponed as the president had agreed to say a few words at the dedication of the new Soldiers' Cemetery in a little town in Pennsylvania. As almost an afterthought, Lincoln invited his Canadian visitor to accompany the presidential party should he so desire. McDougall accepted with thanks and the following day boarded the same train that was to take the president to Gettysburg.

Later that evening, Lincoln excused himself from McDougall and the rest of his dinner guests saying that he had to put some finishing touches on the speech he had been asked to give. Lincoln retired to an ante-room while the conviviality continued.

The next day, the young Canadian, surrounded by a crowd of nearly 15,000, stood in solemn silence as Lincoln began to speak. Just two minutes and 271 words later, Lincoln concluded his dissertation. Though brief and seemingly unremarkable at the time, Lincoln's Gettysburg Address would soon be recognized, along with the Declaration of Independence and Constitution, as one of America's great documents.

Gettysberg Cemetery, 1994.

INSTITUTE OF RENOWN

October 24, 1993

In 1907, RCMI member and prominent Canadian architect Vaux Chadwick designed this "backyard" addition to 245 Simcoe Street, thereby giving the club an impressive University Avenue frontage.

Today's University Avenue is lined with a multitude of modern skyscrapers, most occupied by internationally active insurance corporations, a sprawling network of interconnected hospital buildings, shiny new condominium towers and other contemporary structures, some we admire architecturally, others that simply fade into the background.

But every once in while, this profusion of vertical columns is tamed by remnants of an architectural age long vanished. On the west side of the street, a few steps south of Dundas Street, stands the home of the Royal Canadian Military Institute (RCMI). A pair of ancient muzzle-loading cannon defend its patriarchal position on the busy thoroughfare.

The RCMI was formally established in 1890, though its roots go back another dozen years to a time when a few of Toronto's citizen soldiers met infrequently to discuss the philosophy of war as presented in the various military publications of the day.

It wasn't until the last decade of the nineteenth century that a more permanent organization was formed "to promote military art, science and literature as well as good fellowship." The human inspiration behind the creation of the new Canadian Military Institute (the *Royal* was added in 1948) was the popular and influential Lieutenant-Colonel William Otter of the Queen's Own Rifles who would serve as the CMI's first president.

The organization's first "home" was in a rented building at 94 King Street West where meetings continued to be held until increased membership prompted a move to slightly larger facilities on the Queen Street Avenue (now University Avenue) in a house that stood on the site of the stately Canada Life Building.

Soon the need for increased space necessitated another move and when plans to move into the new Armouries building across the street failed the membership purchased a house on the east side of Simcoe Street, just south of St. Patrick (now Dundas) Street.

There, thanks to the talents of Captain Vaux Chadwick, an architect and member of the institute, an addition was made to the back part of the old house and a new entrance off University Avenue was constructed. Five years went by, the membership roles grew (talk of war was in the air) and in 1912 the building was enlarged once more, this time gaining an appearance that thankfully still graces the busy thoroughfare.

Chadwick enlarged his earlier building five years later, resulting in the RCMI building that's still with us at 426 University Avenue.

PARK PLAZA'S PAST

October 31, 1993

Usually it's easy to find research material for the various subjects I select for each week's *"The Way We Were"* column. Old books in my personal library or those in the Central Reference Library on Yonge Street are a good starting place. Then there are the fascinating articles, usually prepared just as an event occurred, that have been saved for posterity on microfilm in the *Sun* library. Tapping the memories of long-time Torontonians frequently unleashes stories long forgotten. For this week's story, however, I really had to do some digging.

Standing at the northwest corner of Bloor Street and Avenue Road is the stately Park Plaza, now one of the city's finest hotels. But it didn't always enjoy that distinction. People

Original architect's concept for the Queen's Park Plaza apartment hotel in *Financial Post* ad, 1927.

have told me that they remember sixty or so years ago when the future hostelry was simply a towering steel skeleton with an eerie kind of appearance that it retained for years and years.

My first thought was to contact the management of the hotel to get the real story. Unfortunately, with the passage of time and staff, no one employed there at the present time was able to provide any details. Nor apparently were there any archival records.

Nothing daunted, my next excursion was to peer through the old *Telegram* newspaper hoping that when the Park Plaza finally opened in mid-1936 (someone thought) there would be a detailed story about the project. Except for finding a few ads proclaiming that the hotel "will be open July 1" (that ad ran May 20, 1936) followed by a series of notices announcing the official opening of "the popular priced luncheonette and grill of the Park Plaza Residential Hotel"

(July 13), the first supper dance at the Plaza Grill featuring "dinner deluxe - $1.00, $1.25 & $150" and "the music of Enreco Del Greco's Park Plaza Orchestra" (July 20) and a notice advising readers that the "Park Plaza Hotel Offers You More - furnished room $65 per month, unfurnished, proportionally lower" I couldn't find a story on the construction of the hotel anywhere. Until, that is, I checked old editions of the Sun's sister paper, the *Financial Post*.

Park Plaza as it looks today.

In FP's library they too have old editions on microfilm and it was from this source that I was able to piece together what had happened to delay construction resulting in the memories of a "skeleton" standing on the corner.

The concept of "a handsome and spacious residential hotel building," to be known as the Queen's Park Plaza, first came to the business community's attention in 1927 when the United Bond Company ran an ad seeking $875,000 through the issuance of first mortgage bonds that would yield 6 1/2 percent. Money flowed freely in the '20s and work soon began.

Originally, the new hotel was to be a reinforced concrete structure, but it was soon discovered that the exacting building codes in force in Toronto resulted in the necessity for heavier and larger-than-expected columns that severely hampered apartment design and the ability to adjust the size and layout of rental space in the new building. Suddenly, the architects decided on a structural steel building that would be more adaptable to interior space changes.

This change resulted in delays in the approval of plans, acquisition of steel (from a mill in Pittsburgh) and its fabrication (in Walkerville). Then the steel workers went on strike.

With all these delays finally out of the way, an August 3, 1928 report in the Financial Post suggested that the steel work would be complete by the end of the month and the building ready for occupancy by year's end.

Unfortunately, work again fell behind schedule and soon after the Great Depression hit in the fall of 1929 both United Bond and its American parent company went under as did Butler Construction, the company that was building the hotel.

Another six years were to go by before new owners came forward and purchased the unfinished structure for $90,000. In the improving business climate of the mid-30s work on the hotel, that with the passage of time had become known simply as the Park Plaza, was completed.

November 7, 1993

Unless you've just arrived from another planet, you're doubtlessly aware that *Show Boat* is now being staged at the new North York Centre for the Performing Arts.

As spectacular as this Canadian version is, it's certainly not the first time Torontonians have had a chance to see the musical version of Edna Ferber's popular novel about life on a Mississippi river boat in latter years of the nineteenth century.

In fact, the first time *Show Boat* "sailed" into Toronto was just three years after Ferber's book was published in 1926, two years after Florenz Ziegfeld's adaptation of Ferber's book opened at New York City's Ziegfeld Theatre on December 27, 1927, and just weeks after Universal completed the first of a trio of film interpretations of the now classic story.

May 27, 1929 ad informing Torontonians that the "singing, talking" silent film version of *Show Boat* had arrived at the Uptown.

The 1929 movie was a silent, which in itself is unusual considering the fact that sound films were starting to predominate throughout the industry. In an effort to at least appear up to date, Universal added a dialogue/music track on disc totally separate from the film but carefully synchronized with it.

When this *Show Boat* appeared at the Uptown (still going strong) the playhouse's talented producer Jack Arthur had prepared a distinctive musical prelude titled "Songs on the Levee" performed by local musicians Evelyn Geary, Evelyn Cloutier, Harvey Doney and the Uptown Choral Ensemble. It was obviously on the bill to get viewers into the mood.

Ads and reviews in the Toronto newspapers confirm that the film, flickered to life on Saturday, May 25, 1936, and played for a full week "at regular prices [which was] the first time this production has been thus presented," to quote the publicist's press release.

This version of *Show Boat* starred Laura La Plante as Magnolia Hawkes, Joseph Schildkraut as Gaylord Ravenal and Helen Morgan (who some sources state was born here in Toronto ... more on that in a future column) as Julie LaVerne. The crowds were of a sufficient number to prompt the theatre man-

On July 17, 1936, a new *Show Boat* was just a day away.

agement to suggest theatre-goers attend the matinee performances.

Universal's second version was released in 1936 appearing at Toronto's celebrated Tivoli Theatre in mid-July of that year. The Tivoli stood at the southwest corner of Richmond and Victoria intersection. It was built in 1917 as the Allen by the pioneering Canadian movie house entrepreneurs Jules and Jay Allen, the Tivoli (renamed by the new owner Famous Players in 1924) was unique in that it didn't have a balcony. All 1,553 seats were on the main floor, a triumph of engineering technology back then. The theatre closed late 1964 and was soon demolished.

The 1936 *Show Boat* was "crewed" by Irene Dunn as Magnolia, Allan Jones as Ravenal and the immortal Paul "*Old Man River*" Robeson as Joe.

A decade and a half went by and M-G-M got into the act producing a third film version in 1951. This time Kathryn Grayson played Magnolia, Howard Keel was Ravenal, Ava Gardner was Julie and William Warfield portrayed Joe. This *Show Boat* played at the Loew's Theatre, now the lovingly restored Elgin/Wintergarden.

My thanks to the *Sun*'s Jim McPherson for help with this story.

PICTURE THIS

November 14, 1993

With the present year winding down, so too are the various events associated with the 200th anniversary of both the City of York and the City of Toronto. York has evolved from what Simcoe laid out in 1793 as the "Township of York and its peninsula (now Toronto Island)" while Toronto began as the Town of York that occupied a mere thirty acres within that pioneer township.

Many of the events that have taken place during each community's bi-centennial festivities have been captured on film, and years from now will be regarded as valuable resource material for historians of the day.

While photography isn't quite as old as our city, many are surprised to learn that there are photographs of Toronto depicting the young city when it was barely a half-century old. Some of the most intriguing views are those taken in the mid-1850s to supplement a report prepared by city council as it made its "pitch" to become the capital of the Province of Canada. That honour was to go to Ottawa in 1857, that city becoming the capital of the new Dominion of Canada a decade later.

Photography continued to evolve and soon became a popular pastime for many Torontonians. By 1899, this pastime had become popular enough to entice the founder of Kodak, George Eastman, who a few years earlier had invented the roll film camera, to visit Canada from his home in Rochester, New York. He subsequently decided to establish his first "foreign" subsidiary in

The present Kodak Canada complex on Eglinton Avenue West in the
City of York as it appeared during the First World War when part of the
complex was used as a barracks. *(Kodak Canada Archives)*

a building (that still stands) at 41 Colborne Street right in the heart of a young and bustling Toronto. Here Kodak employed ten people cutting and packaging film and photographic paper, fitting lenses to cameras and mixing photographic chemicals.

Business demands soon prompted a move to larger, less congested facilities and in 1901 a large building was constructed on King Street West near Portland. Business continued to grow and by 1908 Kodak's 108 employees were accommodated in a much expanded complex at 588–92 King Street West where the manufacture of film, paper and photographic mounts was now part of day-to-day operations.

Eventually outgrowing the King Street premises, Kodak, under the personal direction of its founder, purchased twenty-five acres of land on the north side of Eglinton Avenue West in the still somewhat rural Township of York. By 1914

Kodak Canada started rather modestly in the building seen in the centre of this photo. The structure at 41 Colborne Street was ten years old when the company began Canadian operations in 1899.

work was well underway on the construction of seven specially designed buildings that made up the new Kodak Heights complex.

Nearly eight decades have gone by since Kodak Canada moved to the company's Eglinton Avenue site. In that period of time, the site has more than doubled in size to fifty-seven acres and accommodates all manufacturing operations (including that of slide and print film, microfilm, specialty photographic products, and so on), administration and marketing offices and distribution facilities for a host of Kodak products.

TORONTO LORE

November 21, 1993

A bunch of this and that for this week's column starting with a story about an interesting piece of "Torontoiana" (if there is such a word) that goes on the block over at Waddington's auction rooms on Queen Street East later this month. It's a small 4 1/4" x 2" snuff box made in 1838 by one of the prisoners being held in the old city jail then

John Brown's snuff box, fabricated in 1838 in the Toronto jail and now up for auction.

situated near the northeast corner of King and Toronto streets.

John Brown, who owned a farm in Pickering Township, was one of the many patriots incarcerated following the ill-fated rebellion led by fiery William Lyon Mackenzie against government officials in December of 1837. While in the Toronto Jail Brown fashioned this small memento for Miss Agnes Lawson (presumably his true love) and, his mind still filled with remorse having witnessed the hanging of his friends Sam Lount and Peter Matthews in the jail yard a few weeks before, inscribed the words on a panel affixed to the box:

Their minds were tranquil and serene,
No terror in their looks were seen,
Their steps upon the scaffold strong,
A moments pause - Their lives are gone.

This historic artifact will be auctioned, along with a framed photo of a relief carving of Captain Matthews by Emanuel Hahn, on the evening of November 30. Call Waddington's for additional details.

On October 25, 1894, Toronto's new Fred Victor Mission opened its doors at the southwest corner of Jarvis and Queen streets. Though new in name, the mission had really been "born" eight years earlier when Mary Sheffield, a devout adherent of Metropolitan Methodist Church on Queen Street East (now Metropolitan United) opened a Sunday School for poor boys in the old Orange Hall across the street from her church. After a shaky start (no one showed up for the school's inaugural gathering) Mary's project soon began to flourish. Eventually, Hart Massey, industrialist and philanthropist extraordi-

123

naire, took an interest in the work of the mission where his son Fred Victor had become a regular volunteer. When Fred died suddenly at the age of only twenty-three, Hart's interest in the mission escalated, so much so that in 1893 he commissioned local architect Edward Lennox to design a modern new facility that, when opened in the fall of the following year, was known as the Fred Victor Mission.

To capture its century of service to our community author Cary Fagan has written a wonderful new book titled *The Fred Victor Mission Story* that's available in hardcover ($24.95) or softcover ($14.95) by mail from the Fred

Fred Victor Massey (1867–90), namesake of Toronto's Fred Victor Mission. *(From* The Fred Victor Mission Story *by Cary Fagan, Wood Lake Books.)*

A 1912 photo of the Victorian Hospital for Sick Children, College Street, that later this week will become the new home of the Canadian Red Cross Toronto and Central Region Blood Centre.

Victor Mission, 145 Queen Street East, Toronto M5A 1S1 (add $3 postage and handling) or at the United Church bookstore, 85 St. Clair Avenue East.

∾

Later this week, the Canadian Red Cross Blood Centre for Toronto and Central Ontario moves into its new headquarters at 67 College Street. In an interesting twist of fate, the Centre's new home is in one of the city's pioneer health services buildings, the former Victorian Hospital for Sick Children that opened in May, 1892, and was abandoned as a hospital when the new Sick Kids on University Avenue opened fifty-nine years later.

The Blood Centre itself has an interesting history. Established in 1949 as the Toronto Blood Centre, the sixth such facility in the Red Cross nationwide system, its first home was located in the now demolished Chorley Park, the one-time home of the province's lieutenant-governor located in north Rosedale. In 1952, the Centre moved into the Canadian Red Cross Society's headquarters at 460 Jarvis Street where it remained until 1973 when it moved to the Michener Institute of Applied Health Services on St. Patrick Street. In 1984 plans to find a new home for the Blood Centre, now one of seventeen such regional centres nationwide, began in earnest. Two years later an agreement was reached with the Toronto Hospital, the owner of 67 College Street, that would see the exterior of the historic structure restored and the interior adapted to house facilities for the collecting, testing, processing and distributing of blood and blood products for more than sixty Canadian hospitals.

STREETCARS ON PARADE

November 28, 1993

Introduced to Torontonians in the fall of 1938, the new Presidents' Conference Committee (PCC) streetcar would go on to distinguish itself as one of the most popular and versatile public transit vehicles ever produced. Nearly 5,000 PCCs saw service in North America with another 15,000 PCCs or cars using PCC patents manufactured in foreign countries.

Torontonians admire their new PCC car at the 1938 CNE. *(TTC)*

Although the TTC has retired most of it's PCCs, a few can still be found helping out during rush hour and in base service on the Harbourfront line operating between Union Station and Spadina Avenue.

The genesis of this type of streetcar can be traced back to the years following the end of the Great War when transit companies in both Canada and the United States began to experience severe declines in ridership. Several factors were responsible for this alarming situation not the least of which was the deplorable condition of the antiquated transit vehicles then in use, many of which were not unlike the types of streetcars introduced at the turn of the century. It was painfully evident that a more comfortable and efficient electric transit vehicle had to be produced.

A meeting of executives of several dozen American transit companies and twenty-six transit-oriented manufacturing concerns convened in Chicago in December of 1929. (For reasons related to tariffs and duties, Toronto and Montreal didn't join the organization until 1933.) At these meetings an organization to be known as the Presidents' Conference Committee (thus the term PCC) was established and given a mandate to develop a totally new street railway vehicle that would address all the problems and concerns facing the beleaguered transit industry. Funding for the project came from levies assessed against each committee member.

After years of research, design work and countless hours of intensive testing of full-size prototype vehicles, car #1009 of the Brooklyn & Queens Transit Corporation became the first PCC to enter revenue service. Depositing the first five-cent fare in the car's fare box that October 1, 1936, was none other than popular New York City Mayor Fiorello La Guardia.

While the PCC was unquestionably a significant improvement over electric transit vehicles then in service, for various reasons initial sales of the car were disappointing with less than 800 of the new cars in operation in 1938, the year that the Toronto Transportation Commission placed the largest order to date for the revolutionary vehicle. Some described the Toronto order as resuscitating a project that was running out of steam.

A total of 140 PCCs (with bodies to be built by the St. Louis Car Company, the trucks by Clark Equipment with electric motors from Canadian Westinghouse in Hamilton and final assembly by Canadian Car and Foundry in Montreal) were ordered in the spring of 1938 at a cost of $3 million (approximately $21,500 per car). Torontonians first saw their new car at that year's CNE and could ride it on the St. Clair route early that fall.

Over the years, the PCC car underwent continual refinement and as it did the TTC continued to expand its PCC fleet by adding 400 more new cars and 205 "used" PCCs from cities like Cincinnati, Cleveland, Birmingham and Kansas City. In total, the TTC has had 745 Presidents' Conference Committee cars on its roster, nineteen of which underwent a major rebuilding program several years ago and can still be seen hard at work on (and under) city streets.

This article was prompted by the recent release of Ray Neilson's newest VHS video titled *PCCs on Parade - America's Heartland.* A delight for any "streetcar connoisseur," this sixty-minute production features rare color footage of PCCs in service in many mid-continent American cities and is a companion video to Ray's earlier effort *PCCs on Parade - The Big East* which includes a segment on Toronto's various PCC models. Both videos ($44.98 each) are available either at George's Trains on Mt. Pleasant Road or from Ray by calling (416) 239-9094.

PCCs are frequently found in rush hour service on various streetcar routes and in regular base service on the Harbourfront line.

Note: Due to complaints from residents who objected to "wheel squeal," PCCs on the Harbourfront line were replaced by Canadian Light Rail Vehicles in October 1994.

A BOOKISH HISTORY

December 5, 1993

This year marks the centennial of one of Toronto's oldest family-owned businesses. The year was 1893 and young Albert Britnell, who had operated a small used and rare book store with his brother John on the west side of Yonge Street south of Agnes Street (now Dundas) since his arrival in Toronto from Chinnor, a small village west of London, England, some nine years earlier, decided to go out on his own.

He set up shop at 240 Yonge Street and called his business, naturally enough, the Albert Britnell Book Shop.

As the years went by Albert's supply of used and rare books, and something he called "Canadiana," grew as did the number of customers visiting the young man's

Albert Britnell, founder of the century-old Britnell's Book Shop.
(Courtesy Mary Britnell Fisher)

shop. It wasn't long before the store's reputation prompted statesmen such as Wilfrid Laurier, Oliver Mowat and a young Mackenzie King to stop by for a visit.

Business prospered and eventually Albert was forced to seek larger quarters and thus began a series of moves to other lower Yonge Street addresses; #254 in 1895, #248 in 1899 and four years later across the street, a few doors north of Shuter at #241, where, that year's city directory advises us, he had a collection of more than 100,000 volumes lining the store's shelves.

A few years later he settled in at #263, which was to be his last downtown Toronto address.

An astute businessman, Albert sensed that commerce was moving uptown and in 1920 he transferred his huge collection of books to a store on the east side of Yonge just north of Collier Street, a location which less than seven decades earlier had been in the Town of Yorkville, the city's original "bedroom suburb."

Eventually Albert's health began to fail and it became necessary for his sixteen-year-old son, Roy, to relinquish his schooling (and any idea of becoming a lawyer) to assume management of the family business. On October 16, 1924, Albert Britnell passed away.

Until now, the Britnell book business had always been located in a shop owned by someone else, its interior shape, size and amenities predetermined by the existing space. That would soon change, for in 1927 Roy purchased a lot on the east side of Yonge just steps north of the busy Bloor corner. Over the next twelve months Roy supervised the construction of a new store in a new building, one complete with space-saving adjustable shelving (on which books were arranged, each volume within the potential customer's easy reach), vast amounts of storage space for vast numbers of books in the basement, a freight elevator to facilitate the stocking of the shelves and a special area at the front of the store where, for the first time, new books, now absolutely essential to assure the survival of book stores, were offered for sale. Roy's office and his treasured Canadiana volumes were to be found at the back of the store.

In 1956 young Barry, Roy's son, joined the staff to ease the burden on his aging father. Sadly, Barry passed away in 1980 and Roy just three years later. Today a fourth generation of Britnell's, Betsy and Jordan, ably assisted by their mother and Barry's widow, Mary, carry on the century-old tradition at the 765 Yonge Street location. And even with the

The Yonge and Bloor intersection (looking north) a few years before Roy built the present Britnell Book Shop that still stands at 765 Yonge Street. *(CTA)*

arrival of the new "chain" book stores, Britnell's continues to maintain its status as one of those special Toronto places.

∾

Reader Doris Morton writes to ask if anyone remembers the location of La Salle Park, a popular picnic ground for many Toronto company outings a half-century ago. If you know where that park was located drop me a note and I'll pass the info on to Doris.

This question solicited dozens of replies from my readers, many of whom recalled fond memories of visiting this small park on the north shore of Hamilton Harbour. Incidentally the park, which was named after the famous seventeenth-century French explorer whose travels brought him into the area, is still there.

PROFUSION OF PLAYHOUSES

January 2, 1994

The modern-day Metro Toronto is blessed with a multitude of fine theatres and playhouses to which hundreds of thousands make their way each year to view both motion pictures and live theatrical performances. While many may believe that this profusion of playhouses (a list that includes the stately Royal Alexandra, Pantages, the stacked Loew's (now the Elgin/Winter Garden duo) and the recently constructed Princess of Wales and the North York Centre for the Performing Arts) is a new phenomenon, a look at the Toronto of seventy or more years ago reveals that even back then an abundant supply of quality theatrical venues was an important feature of the city's social consciousness.

Theatre impresario Jerry Shea.
(Photo courtesy Danny Shea)

Today we can thank, in great measure, people like "Honest Ed" Mirvish, his son David Mirvish and Garth Drabinsky for the return of the "great" theatres and playhouses to our community. Interestingly, these three fellows can, in many ways, be described as modern-day reincarnations of one Jeremiah Shea, Toronto's pioneer theatre impresario. Recently it was my good fortune to meet Danny Shea, Jeremiah's grandson, and he was able to provide me with many details concerning this amazing gentleman's influence on Toronto's theatre heritage.

Jerry Shea (Jeremiah was saved for state occasions and the like) was born in Buffalo, New York, in 1871. Following a brief period in the city school system, Jerry left to assist his older brother, Michael, in the latter's successful vaudeville house business. In 1899, Jerry left Buffalo to open a theatre north of the border and within a few months Toronto's first Shea's Theatre opened on lower Yonge Street, a few steps north of King. Featured that first evening were comedians, jugglers, singers and a clutch of talented cats and dogs. Soon to come were flea circuses, freak shows and touring aboriginal groups, not to mention the odd beauty pageant.

Ten years into the new century, Jerry Shea built a new theatre not far away

Shea's Hippodrome ad.

at the southeast corner of Richmond and Victoria streets naming it, appropriately, Shea's Victoria. A few weeks later he sold the Yonge Street theatre to devote all his resources to booking the new playhouse not just with live talent, but with the newest form of mass entertainment, moving pictures.

As successful as his Victoria was, Jerry Shea wanted something better, and bigger. On April 27, 1914, the 2,700-seat Shea's Hippodrome on the west side of Teraulay Street (as Bay Street north of Queen was then known) welcomed its first patrons. This massive theatre boasted a number of features: it was fire-proof, the interior was decorated in the Renaissance style with Empire features and it was the largest theatre in the country. Of particular interest was the Hippodrome's unique German-built "orchestrion," a mechanical contraption described in the newspaper ads as "the invisible symphony orchestra." With the flick of a switch it could produce the sound of any musical instrument or be made to sound like the entire orchestra.

Like the Victoria, the Hippodrome presented both vaudeville acts as well as "the latest in leading photoplays," the latter known as "chasers" to those in the know, skillfully selected to chase the audience out of the building so a new paying crowd could enter.

Some of the performers who performed on the immense Hippodrome stage in the theatre's early years included George Burns and Gracie Allen, the Four Marx Brothers (Groucho even sings about his visit to Toronto on one of his records (remember them?), Houdini, Toronto's own Walter Huston, Fanny Brice, Milton Berle, Ethel Waters, Bill "Bojangles" Robinson and some guy named Red Skelton. Wonder what ever happened to him?

Not long after Canada declared war on Germany (for the second time) the Hippodrome scrapped its vaudeville program to concentrate on movies, the most popular of which was the 1941 feature "Buck Privates." Abbott and Costello could be seen on the theatre's huge screen for a total of fourteen consecutive weeks.

Jerry Shea died at his Hudson Drive residence in 1943, his remains interred in Mt. Hope Cemetery. Though Jerry had passed away his Toronto theatres lived on. Then in 1956, with the announcement that the city would get a new municipal building and civic square on land opposite the present city hall, the fate of the Hippodrome was sealed. On Monday, December 31, 1956 the house lights dimmed and the grand old theatre's doors were locked for the last time. Within a few months Jerry Shea's Hippodrome was no more.

Shea's headstone in Toronto's Mt. Hope Cemetery.

OFF TO THE RACES

January 9, 1994

On the last day of last year a sporting event that over a span of nearly 200 years had attracted hundreds of thousands of spectators came to an end in the City of Toronto. On that day horse racing in Toronto came to an end. Now, before someone begins composing a "Dear Editor" letter, please note that the statement was "in the *city* of Toronto." The "sport of kings" continues to attract huge crowds to the beautiful Woodbine Race Track in Etobicoke. As far as the city of Toronto is concerned Friday, December 31, 1993, marked the last day of horse racing at the city's legendary Greenwood track.

Historically, the first race course in Toronto was established on the Island by military personnel shortly after they were transferred to the provincial capital in the early years of the last century. To be absolutely precise that course was actually laid out on what was still called *the peninsula* (the geographical term "island" wasn't applied until a savage storm in 1858 breached the narrow isthmus at the east end freeing the wispy fingers of land from the city) opposite the Town of York, city status and name change not being accorded the community until March 6 of 1834. This race course wasn't public but reserved almost exclusively for the use of the military.

Of the first "public" race course, there is only a brief reference in John Ross Robertson's encyclopedic *Landmarks of Toronto* in which he records that horse racing was held along Front Street from Small's Corner (today's Berkeley Street) to the market.

For a number of years in the mid-1830s the land between the New and Old Forts (Stanley Barracks and Fort York) became the site of frequent races under the patronage of several senior military officers.

The first real race course, that is, one with stands for the spectators and a properly groomed track, was the Simcoe Chase Course (also known as Scarlett's) located on the north side of Dundas Street just east of the Humber River and operated by John Scarlett (thus Scarlett Road) who lived in a nearby dwelling he called Runnymede (thus Runnymede Road). This facility opened in the fall of 1837.

It was followed in 1841 or '42 by the Boulton Race Course that occupied land bounded by today's Spadina, Bloor, McCaul and Baldwin streets. Then followed by Maitland's "over the Don" south and west of the Queen and Broadview intersection.

Succeeding Jack Maitland's place was Nelson Gate's race course several miles out what was then referred to as the Don and Danforth Road. Today, this course along with several other internationally known English race courses,

Newmarket, Gatwick, Doncaster and Epsom, are remembered in the names of streets in the Danforth Avenue - Main Street neighbourhood.

In 1857, the next in a myriad of Toronto race tracks opened. This one, called Carlton because of its proximity to the small village of Carlton, was located in the western outskirts of the city just south of Dundas Street and a few yards west of a narrow tree-lined concession road. The owner of this course gave his name both to the track and to the concession road. W.C. Keele was a prominent businessman in west Toronto and it was at his course, in 1860, that the Queen's Plate was awarded for the first time. Another rather obscure record is held by this course. It was at the Carlton course that the running of the 1860 edition of something called the Scurry Stakes was won by an eight-year-old jockey.

In 1874, a new course opened out the Kingston Road (as Queen Street east of the Don River was known). It was operated by Messrs. Pardee and Howell who had purchased the southern portion of Joseph Duggan's country estate. The pair decided to develop a race course the name of which was taken from Howell's hotel at 88 Yonge Street, the Woodbine House.

Things didn't go quite the way Pardee and Howell had hoped and the property eventually reverted back to the original owner, Mr. Duggan. Under his encouragement, and that of the newly established Ontario Jockey Club, Woodbine (changed to "Old" Woodbine in 1956 and Greenwood seven years later) was to become one of the continent's most popular tracks and a true Toronto landmark.

The present idea to turn the site into a housing development was first broached in 1941, if you think that it's a new idea.

In 1951, the City of Toronto Planning Department envisioned this residential development on the Woodbine track site, view looking east from Coxwell. Keating Street Extension is today's Lake Shore Boulevard East.

AJAX BORN IN WAR BOOM

January 16, 1994

A few weeks ago I was saddened to read that William McLean had passed away at the age of just fifty-eight. While I had never met Mr. McLean personally, I felt I knew him because of a very nice letter he sent me in 1985. Back then Bill McLean was the mayor of Ajax (a position he held from 1980 to 1988) and when I forwarded a letter to town officials requesting information on the history of the community, Mayor Bill took time out of his busy schedule to respond to my enquiry, personally, adding some nice comments about this column to boot. I wish now that I had taken the time to meet and chat with Bill about the growth of Ajax. The best I can do now is to respectfully dedicate this column to his memory.

In relative terms, the history of Ajax, Ontario, a town twenty-three miles east of Toronto, is short, spanning a little more than half a century. (Interestingly, to me at least, is the fact that the town is the same age as I am.)

Prior to 1941, the future site of today's modern Ajax was nothing more than acres and acres of rolling farm fields located in the southernmost reaches of the ancient Township of Pickering. In that same year, the federal government, through a concern known as Defence Industries Limited (DIL), established a sprawling munitions plant that was soon turning out huge quantities of much-needed anti-aircraft and mortar shells plus other types of ammunition for the allied war effort. The new plant covered almost 3,000 acres of former farm land stretching from Duffins Creek on the west to Pickering Beach Road on the east and from just south of Highway 2 to the lakefront. The property was purchased from pioneer farm families for an average $125 an acre.

In mid-March 1942, the community surrounding the busy defence plant was elevated to the status of incorporated village and it soon became apparent that the place needed a name, something better than the unofficial and rather unflattering DILCO. Allied military victories were few and far between in the early days of the war so it was only natural that when the German pocket battleship *Graf Spee* was scuttled off the coast of Uruguay on December 17, 1939, the names of the three vessels responsible for its destruction, HMNZS *Achilles,* HMS *Exeter* and HMS *Ajax* would be on everyone's lips. The people at DILCO took it a step further christening their small, but proud, war-born community after the latter warship. This connection with HMS *Ajax* was to remain strong. Its main street, Harwood, is named in honour of Henry H. Harwood, Commander of the British flotilla at the Battle of the River Plate. Other town streets have been named for crewmen of the *Ajax,* eleven of which (Bashford, Burrells, Clements, Ellems, Farley, Follett, Frankcom, Hills,

Lambart, Meek, Plowman and Smith) were killed in action during the *Graf Spee* engagement.

In its four years of operation, the DIL plant, which was to develop into the largest of its kind in the British Empire, produced approximately forty-four million shells.

With victory in Europe and in the Pacific close at hand, the problem of what to do with the huge Ajax munitions complex, including the numerous ancillary buildings where the vast majority of the organization's 9,000 or so war workers from all across Canada spent their "off-duty" hours, soon became a major concern.

Fortunately, a use was on the horizon. Huge numbers

The old DILCO sign, by which CNR trainmen identified the war-time munitions community, was turned over to Ajax Mayor William Parrish at a special ceremony in October 1963.
(Toronto Telegram *photo from* Toronto Sun *library*)

of military personnel returning from foreign battlefields and eager to continue their education enrolled at the University of Toronto. To help overcome the strain on the school's campus in the heart of the big city, Ajax was transformed into a dynamic university town. Those structures "infected" with residual explosive material were demolished with most of the other structures converted to educational facilities. During the hectic post-war years of 1946 through 1949, almost 7,000 engineering students were enrolled at the U of T's Ajax Division.

School was out, literally, in 1949 but by now many hundreds had come to call Ajax home, and in 1950 the Ontario Municipal Board decreed that the community would henceforth be the Corporation of the Improvement District of Ajax under the watchful eyes of a trio of trustees. Three years later, full town status was achieved under Mayor Benjamin de Forest Bayly (for whom Bayly Street was named).

Though the last three decades have altered the Ajax scene tremendously, the 55,000 citizens of this proud community continue to revere their history thanks in great measure to the efforts of the late Bill McLean.

A PENNY SAVED

January 23, 1994

When we think of banks here in Canada (the money kind, not those of a watercourse), invariably we think of the nine so-called "domestic" banks; T-D, Montreal, Royal, etc., the newest in that list being the Manulife Bank. In actual fact, Canadians have a choice of sixty-one different banks, the aforementioned domestic chartered banks plus another fifty-two schedule "II" foreign bank subsidiaries (including Mitsubishi Bank of Canada, Korea Exchange Bank of Canada, Israel Discount Bank of Canada and Fuji Bank Canada).

One of the most interesting banks to serve the citizens of our community, and one that's now just a fond memory for many Ontarians, was the Penny Bank that was established in the early years of this century to encourage thrift amongst school children which, it was hoped, would lead to thrift in later life. In those days government handouts were unknown and for many depositors their savings in the Penny Bank (and accumulated interest) frequently meant the difference between the family going hungry and a nourishing meal.

The Penny Bank of Toronto was established in 1904 through the amalgamation of two existing institutions, the Savings Association of St. Andrew's Presbyterian Church and the Victor Five-Cent Savings Association, the latter affiliated with the Fred Victor Mission at Queen and Jarvis streets, a remarkable community treasure now in its 100th year of service. For hundreds of the city's less affluent citizens the service provided by these institutions was a true blessing since the large established banks required a minimum deposit of one dollar, a sum unattainable for many.

The idea of providing an opportunity for school children to save their pennies (and earn interest) was pioneered by the Victor organization about 1900 when it made arrangements with the Board of Education to offer the pupils of Lord Dufferin School their own bank. Encouraged by Trustee C.A.B. Brown (for whom Brown School was named) the venture was a resounding success and eventually led to the creation of an organization that makes penny banking available to all city public schools.

This organization was known as the Penny Bank of Toronto and was created by an act of the provincial government on April 19, 1904 (interestingly, the very day the city's downtown core was nearly obliterated by a raging fire). The new bank went into business on April 3 of the following year.

The building selected to house the bank's office was the York Street Public School at the northwest corner of York and Richmond streets (now a park-

ing lot) that had wel-
comed its first pupils
in 1870. It was here
that the money col-
lected by the teachers
every Monday morn-
ing was transferred.

Over the first few
years of the bank's exis-
tence some 30,000
accounts were opened
with pupils making
nearly 400,000 deposits
each of which averaged
twenty cents. The bank
paid 3 percent interest
on the deposits. In 1923,
the Penny Bank spread
to other Ontario schools
and the name of the
organization was

From its beginning in 1904, the administrative
offices of the Penny Bank were located in the old
York Street School at the northwest corner of York
and Richmond streets seen here in a 1922 photo. In
later years the bank moved to the Board of Education
offices at Orde and McCaul streets. The bank went
"out of business" in 1947.

changed to the Penny Bank of Ontario.

The bank's success led many teachers to complain that its activities were
getting in the way of trying to educate the students and several attempts
were made to terminate the bank. So strong were its roots, however, that
the Penny Bank continued for another two decades. Peak participation
occurred in early 1940 with 532 schools province-wide taking part in the
program and a total of $1,528,000 on deposit.

As the war in Europe and the Pacific intensified, officials felt that a better
use for the children's pennies, nickels and dimes was to have them invested
in War Savings Stamps, and in early February 1943 the Penny Bank suspended operations. In 1947 directors of the bank requested that the government take steps to dissolve the entire operation. Part of the dissolution
process saw individual accounts, each with more than one dollar on
deposit, transferred to the Post Office Savings Bank. A total of 13,000
accounts, totalling $51,046, went to the Post Office.

When all the bank's liabilities were disbursed the remaining money was
turned over to the Hospital for Sick Children. A brief news story in the
October 2, 1948, edition of the Evening Telegram reported that a young
polio patient at the hospital had accepted, on behalf of the hospital, a
cheque for $101,941.14 thereby concluding all affairs related to the Penny
Bank.

IT'S ALL OVER FOR FIVE AND DIMES

January 30, 1994

Woolworth's store was a landmark at the northwest corner of Yonge and Queen streets from 1912 until its closure in 1979. Loew's up the street is now the Elgin and the Yonge streetcars were replaced by subway trains sixteen years after this photo was taken in 1938. *(TTC)*

Many of us still refer to The Bay's downtown Toronto store as Simpson's even though the 119-year-old Simpson name ceased to exist as a Canadian retail outlet in June of 1991.

Well, here we go again. Within the next few months an equally familiar name, a name that's been familiar to Canadian shoppers for almost as long as the Simpson title, will also vanish. And when that day arrives no longer will the red and gold letters that spell out F.W. Woolworth be seen on the hundreds of stores that for decades formed an integral part of business life in Canadian cities and towns from coast to coast.

At the same time, Woolworth's retail colleague, Woolco, a discount department-style store created by the parent company in 1962, will also

A large Woolworth store was wrapped around the Tamblyn drug store
(that name's gone too) at the northwest corner of Yonge Street and
Eglinton Avenue, 1965.

vanish. The majority of Woolco outlets will be taken over by Wal-Mart, a
company that, co-incidentally, was also born in 1962.

Though the Woolworth and Woolco retail outlets will vanish, the
Woolworth company itself will continue to be one of the country's largest
retail conglomerates through the operation of specialty shops like Foot
Locker, Northern Reflections, Randy River and a host of others.

∾

Frank Winfield Woolworth was born on a farm in upper New York state in
1854. It took a while, but eventually young Frank escaped the back-break-
ing, dawn-to-dusk routine of farm work and gained employment in a small
Watertown variety store. At first, Frank worked for free simply to gain some
business experience. After three months, he was offered the munificent sum
of $3.50 per week. Saving every cent he could, the ambitious Woolworth
decided to open his own store where all items offered for sale cost just a
nickel.

His first attempt, a small unpretentious place in Utica, started off well,
but soon fell on hard times. Woolworth retreated back to Watertown only
to try again a few months later with a store in Lancaster, Pennsylvania. This
time things clicked and eventually a "dime table" was added.

As the years passed additional Woolworth "five & dime" stores opened and soon "F.W." began eyeing the lucrative Canadian market.

His sights were set on Toronto.

Woolworth's cousin, Seymour Horace Knox, had opened a five and dime variety store in Phil Jameson's building at the northwest corner of Yonge and Queen streets (a structure that still stands with the site of Knox's store now occupied by a branch of the Royal Bank) in 1897. A native of Buffalo, New York (Seymour's descendants continue their Buffalo presence as owners of the Sabres NHL hockey team) Knox modelled his new Toronto store on the one he owned in Erie, Pennsylvania.

Frank Winfield Woolworth
(1854–1919).

In 1912, cousins Knox and Woolworth, plus several other American pioneers in the "five and dime" chain store business – Messrs. Kirby, Charlton and Moore – pooled their collective resources and talents and created the F.W. Woolworth chain of stores. One condition of the merger was that the new chain bear the name of the majority shareholder. It was through this merger that Woolworth was able to enter the Canadian market.

A few days after the appropriate documents were endorsed by all participants, the S.H. Knox sign at the corner of Toronto's Yonge and Queen streets came down and up went Frank's red and gold letters. Woolworth's had arrived to Canada.

Now, 82 years later, the Woolworth signs are coming down.

AUTOMANIA

February 6, 1994

Later this month the 21st edition of the Canadian International Autoshow will be featured at the Metro Toronto Convention Centre and SkyDome complex. When the show was first held back in 1974 only six auto manufactures (GM, Ford, Chrysler, AMC, Datsun and Toyota) were featured and the exhibits occupied less than 85,000 square feet out at the sprawling International Centre. This year forty manufacturers from thirteen different countries representing virtually all segments of the automotive industry will present their offerings dispersed over half a million square feet of exhibit space.

The idea of presenting the newest in automobile styles and technology at a car show has been a feature of our city for almost as long as Torontonians have been in love with the "horseless carriage."

While researching my recently published book *From Horse Power to Horsepower*, which offers the reader a look at the changing modes of transportation in our city from 1890 to 1930, it became evident that the first people to take advantage of automobile exhibitions were the auto dealers themselves. Toronto's turn-of-the-century auto dealers frequently presented their newest offerings at what they arbitrarily called a motor show, a display invariably held

The sparkling new Automotive Building at the CNE was erected in the remarkable short span of just 138 days. It was opened August 23, 1929. *(CNE)*

right in the showroom. Obviously, under these conditions, the public only saw the makes and models offered for sale by individual dealers.

It wasn't until March 31, 1906, that a motor show featuring a truly representative variety of makes and models was held in the old Granite Club building on Church Street. Grandly titled the Canadian Automobile and Motor Boat Show, the event was formally opened by the lieutenant-governor of the day, Mortimer Clark, accompanied by a clutch of elected provincial and civic officials.

That the event was destined to be a success is evident from an *Evening Telegram* report that appeared in the paper opening day:
All the space in the 2 rinks has been fully taken up and during the past week the management have been obliged to refuse space to some manufactures. The rinks are decorated with flags and bunting and will have a pretty appearance when the show is opened.

A nearby ad said it all: "$400,000 worth of 1906 triumphs. Greatest display of Automobiles, Motor Boats, Marine Engines and accessories ever seen in Canada."

Rather ominously, another ad on the same page implored the reader not to buy a car until they had looked them over at "the Real Big Automobile Show" scheduled to be held a week or so later at the Mutual Street Rink. At this rival motor show, French and British makes such as De Dion, Panhard, Daimler, Napier, Triumph and Argyle were to be featured.

Some years later the Toronto Motor Show was organized and it presented exhibitions in the University Avenue Armouries (located where the Court House now stands), and after 1909 in the new Transportation Building at the CNE (a building that as the Spanish Pavilion burned to the ground in 1974). It was in this latter building that Frederick Fetherstonhaugh's battery-powered car, which had been demonstrated at the 1893 Exhibition making it one of the world's first electric cars, was put on display in 1912.

It appears that the Toronto Show then became the National Motor Show of Canada that in February of 1929 was held on the upper four floors of the newly constructed eight-storey addition to the Robert Simpson store at Bay and Richmond streets. The large cars were elevated to and lowered from the upper display floors using crane, block and tackle positioned on Bay Street.

Later that year, the new $1 million Automotive Building at the CNE was officially opened by Ontario Premier Howard Ferguson. For almost four decades, the car show was the most popular event presented at the annual fair. It was here that fair-goers saw the newest cars and trucks including the revolutionary *Tucker* in 1947 and the ill-starred Ford *Edsel* ten years later. Then, because new car introduction dates began to take place after the fair had ended, it was decided to discontinue the CNE Auto Show in 1967.

DISTINGUISHED WAR SERVICE

February 13, 1994

Regular readers of this column will be aware of my fascination with the part played by citizens of British North America in the bloody civil war that saw the untimely deaths of more than 600,000 during the period of 1861 to 1865. In fact, several sources have suggested that as many as 50,000 individuals from north of the border took part in the four-year conflict, some siding with the Union forces in an effort to help abolish slavery, others with the Confederacy fearing that the Union would attempt to overrun the British provinces once the southern states had been defeated.

Many noted historians have concluded that this latter possibility prompted the young provinces to affect an alliance that would culminate a little more than two years after the war's conclusion on April 9, 1865, at Appomattox Courthouse, Virginia, in the confederation of Upper and Lower Canada, Nova Scotia and New Brunswick, creating the new Dominion of Canada.

While the total number of British North Americans wearing either the "blue" or "grey" has yet to be authenticated, there's lit-

A proud Dr. Anderson Abbott in his Union Army uniform.
(Metro Toronto Public Library, courtesy Cathy Slaney)

tle doubt that whatever the number many were from Toronto. Several, including John Tomlinson, James Knowlton and Charles Bolton, had their civil war experiences documented in lengthy newspaper obituaries. The latter gentleman formed the subject of my March 1, 1992 *"The Way We Were"* column that was reprinted in Toronto Sketches (Dundurn Press, 1992).

Recently, thanks to Cathy Slaney who lives in Georgetown, Ontario, I learned about another Torontonian who experienced both the joy of comradeship and the terror of battle while serving in the Union's medical corps. And Dr. Abbott could claim another distinction. He was one of only eight black doctors to serve in the ranks of the Union Army.

Anderson Ruffin Abbott was born in the City of Toronto (population 10,871) on April 17, 1837, just three years after the little community had shaken off its meager town status and mere months before William Lyon Mackenzie was to conduct his own "civil war" in an unsuccessful attempt to oust the provincial government of the day.

Abbott was educated at the Toronto Academy, forerunner of the present Knox College. In those far-off days, the Academy was located on the north side of Front Street where, many years later, the new Royal York Hotel would be erected. After a three-year stint at a school in Ohio, Abbott returned to Toronto where, after more years of study, he graduated at the age of twenty-three, earning another distinction, that of becoming the country's first black doctor.

The good doctor's grave marker in the Necropolis.

Enraged by the vicious kidnapping of runaway slaves who had made their way into Canada via the underground railway, Abbott offered his services to the Union, and in 1863 was appointed surgeon in the U.S. Army. He was later put in charge of Camp Baker and Freedman's Hospitals in Washington, D.C. It was while assigned to the capital district that Abbott met Abraham Lincoln and the two were to become steadfast friends. Following the president's assassination at Ford's Theatre just five days after the war ended,

At a special presentation in Toronto civil war re-enactment soldiers Paul Culliton and Alex Morgan guard the shawl given to Dr. Abbott by President Lincoln.

Mrs. Lincoln presented the doctor with the shawl worn by Lincoln during his first inauguration ceremony.

In later years, Dr. Abbott served in various medical capacities in both Canada and in the United States, ending his distinguished career as Medical Superintendent of Chicago's Provident Hospital.

Anderson Ruffin Abbott died on December 29, 1913, and is buried in the Toronto Necropolis.

TORONTO, WHERE?

February 20, 1994

I, for one, have had enough of all this cold and snow. Everyone into the bus. I'm going to take all my readers to another Toronto where it's warmer. No, we're not off to Toronto, South Dakota, or to Toronto, Illinois, or even to nearby Toronto, Ohio. That last one is just across the river from Pittsburgh. That trio of Torontos is no doubt colder or snowier than our Toronto. Nope, we're off to the sunny south ... to Toronto, Florida.

Cover of the Excelsior Land Investment & Building Company's promotional brochure for the Toronto Estate in Australia.

Oh, by the way. There's no need to make motel or hotel reservations. That's because Toronto, Florida, doesn't have any hotels or motels ... or places to swim ... or even places to eat. In fact, all Toronto, Florida, does have is a highway bridge, two sets of railway tracks and a railway crossing.

Actually, its precisely because of those two sets of tracks that Florida has a Toronto at all. Or should I say had a *Toronto*. All modern references to the "sunshine state's" Toronto have long since vanished.

The origin of the "Toronto-that-might-have-been" goes back to 1866 when one Henry Sweetapple, a Toronto, Ontario-born engineer working for one of Florida's pioneer railway companies, the Florida Central & Peninsular Railway (FC&P), suggested that where the FC&P tracks connecting Jacksonville and Tampa crossed a narrow dirt path just south of the tiny hamlet of Piedmont, Florida (and not far from the orange groves surrounding Orlando) would be the perfect site for a new town sometime in the future. He took the opportunity to christen the remote location Toronto after his hometown. He even took the time to jot that name down in his dusty notebook. The FC&P eventually became part of the much larger Seaboard Air Line Railway.

Some years later another pioneer railway, the South Florida, laid tracks from Sanford to Port Tampa and where they crossed the FC&P line near Piedmont, officials of both railway companies declared that the crossing would retain Sweetapple's designation and the location became known as Toronto.

The South Florida eventually became part of the Atlantic Coast Line Railroad. In 1967, the Atlantic Coast Line and Seaboard Air Line merged to form the present Seaboard Coast Line Railroad that still operates freight trains through the Toronto crossing that's now safely located under a modern concrete highway overpass.

∾

By the way, there is another Toronto that's nice and warm this time of year (in fact, at all times of the year) but we can't get to this one by bus. This Toronto is in New South Wales, Australia. Located between Sydney and Newcastle on the west shore of Lake Macquarrie, this Toronto started as "a mission for the Australian aborigines" established in 1826 by the Rev. Lancelot Threlkeld who was acting on behalf of the London (England) Missionary Society.

Threlkeld's mission, which covered almost 1,300 acres, was abandoned two years later, though the good reverend stayed on developing his own settlement which he called Ebenezer. Some years later coal was discovered on the property and a mine opened. Eventually, the mining of cannel coal was phased out and the site was purchased by the Excelsior Land Investment and Building Company who promptly announced plans to develop a tourist resort.

It was also revealed that the project would have a new name, one that would pay tribute to the hometown of visiting sculler Ned Hanlan who, on August 16, 1884, had been defeated twice by Australian William Beach during spirited races on Sydney's

Paramatta River. Seems that Ned, in spite of losing the two events, had captured the hearts of the Australians. To capitalize on Ned's fame the company decided to call their new development Toronto.

Since the article appeared I discovered Henry Sweetapple's grave in Necropolis, while preparing for a walking tour through that fascinating old cemetery. The headstone reveals that Henry died in Florida on August 26, 1886.

Not far from Orlando, Florida, a slow freight shunts through a rail crossing that Henry Sweetapple envisioned as the site of a future Toronto.

HAPPY 160TH TORONTO!

March 6, 1994

If you're looking for a reason to party today, here's a good one. It was exactly 160 years ago today, March 6, 1834, that the little community of York, Upper Canada (now Ontario) was elevated to the exalted rank of city, the first of that status in the province's short history. By the same decree, and as a result of a vote of 22 to 12, the community's name was changed back to the original Toronto. Overnight the 9,254 *Yorkers* became 9,254 *Torontonians*.

In honor of Toronto's 160th anniversary I thought readers might be interested in exploring our community as it was described in the "Commercial Directory, Street Guide and Register," an extremely rare little booklet published by Thomas Dalton at his *Patriot* newspaper office, 233 King Street. The date of publication is just one year prior to the city's incorporation year and describes what Toronto was like in appearance in its very first year. The comments in brackets are mine.

York, the capital of Upper Canada, is beautifully situated near the head of Lake Ontario on the north side of an excellent harbour. York Harbour (one of the very few times the body of water was called anything but Toronto Harbour) *is an elliptical basin of an area of 8 or 9 square miles formed by a long sandy peninsula* (the present Eastern Gap had yet to be formed) *stretching from the land east of the town to a point called Gibraltar Point* (near the present Hanlan's Point)

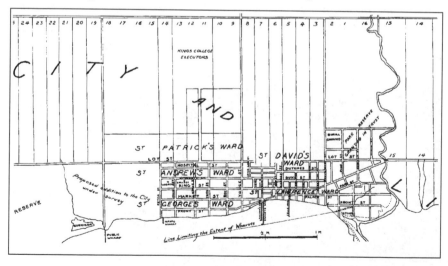

Map of the newly incorporated City of Toronto. *(From Bruce West's* TORONTO, *published by Doubleday Canada, 1979)*

abreast of the present fort (Fort York) *where the troops are stationed. The bay is about 3 miles across having a small river, the Don, emptying into it at the east end.*

On the Peninsula, or Island as it is generally called Mr. Knott has lately erected a manufactory for making starch, soap etc., attached to which is a hotel for the accommodation of parties of pleasure visiting the Island and for whose convenience in getting there a boat has been established propelled by horses (the steeds walked on treadmills that in turn were connected through a set of gears to side paddles).

The town of York is laid out at right angles, the streets are spacious. The main street, called King Street (named in honor of George III, the reigning monarch in 1793 the year York

York as seen from the peninsula in 1828, just six years before the town became the City of Toronto.
(Metro Toronto Library, John Ross Robertson Collection)

Toronto from the Island, 1993.

was established by John Simcoe) *runs through the centre of town from east to west and is one and a half miles in length. The side-paths* (sidewalks) *are well flagged* with stone (the following year some 476 yards of wooden planking was laid) *and an act was passed last Session for macadamizing* (a form of stone pavement) *the street.*

The houses are partly built of wood, but many of them are of brick or stone. York contains the public buildings of the province, viz. the new Parliament Buildings (Front Street West on the site of the new CBC building), *the Government House* (now the site of Roy Thomson Hall), *the College of Upper Canada* (northwest corner of King and Simcoe streets), *the hospital* (northwest corner of King and John streets), *the Upper Canada Bank* (northeast corner of Adelaide and George streets), *the Court House and Gaol* (northwest corner King and Church streets), *a splendid hall called Osgoode Hall for the Law Society* (in 1833 only the east wing had been completed), *a newly erected handsome stone church of the Church of England establishment* (rebuilt twice after fires with the present St. James' Cathedral opening in 1853), *a Roman Catholic church* (St. Paul's on Queen Street East), *and many other churches and chapels belonging to the different religious persuasions.*

The Barracks (Fort York) *are situated at the west end of town with a battery* (cannon) *which protects the entrance to the harbour.* (At that time the only entrance to the bay was through the old West Gap situated several hundred yards north of the present western channel.)

The only outlets from the town are Yonge Street to the north leading through the villages of Vaughan, Markham, Thornhill, etc., to Newmarket and Lake Simcoe. The outlet from the town to the east is called the Kingston Road crossing the Don River about a mile from the town (the present Queen Street, commencing at the east bank of the Don and today's Kingston Road were both part of the Kingston Road back then) *over a handsome bridge built by the present governor* (lieutenant-governor) *Sir John Colborne* (after whom the thoroughfares Colborne and Seaton – he was also Lord Seaton – are named).

The outlet to the west is Lot Street (now Queen) continued by Dundas Street (via today's Ossington Avenue and Dundas Street West) crossing the River Humber 7 miles from the town.

∿

One of the most interesting subjects covered in Walton's little book is found in a chapter titled *Taxation in Upper Canada* where it's stated that *the local taxes or district rates are collected from each individual according to the quantity of land and other property he may possess. The rate of assessment is one penny on the pound.*

> *Assessed values as fixed by law:*
>
> *Every town lot* *£50*
> *Every house built with timber*
> *squared or hewed on 2 sides,*
> *of 1 story, with not more*
> *than 2 fireplaces.* *£20*
> *As above, every additional fireplace* *£4*
> *Every brick or stone house of*
> *1 story and not more than 2 fireplaces* *£40*
> *Every framed, brick or stone house*
> *of 2 stories and not more than 2 fireplaces* *£60*
> *Every additional fireplace* *£10*
> *Every horse of the age 3 years and up* *£8*
> *Every wagon kept for pleasure* *£15*

TRANSIT GOES UNDERGROUND

March 20, 1994

As I sit here at my computer enthusiastically inputing this column, the Rogers (where have I heard that name recently?) cable channel is carrying Metro Council's debate over how many of the proposed new rapid transit lines – Eglinton West subway (Spadina subway to York City centre), Spadina subway (extension to York University), Sheppard subway (Yonge to Don Mills Road) and Scarborough RT (extension to Sheppard) – should be built. After hours of debate construction of both the Eglinton West and Sheppard lines, a total of almost seven miles of new subway, was approved at a cost of nearly $2 billion.

Subway visionary Horatio C. Hocken.

Deciding to construct subways in Toronto has never been an easy thing to do. In fact, subjecting the idea to long, drawn-out periods of discussion has become sort of, how should I put it, a tradition.

Let's go back to the fall of 1909 when talk of building what would have been Toronto's first subway was first promoted.

The idea evolved as a direct result of the unsatisfactory public transit service being provided by the privately owned Toronto Railway Company (TRC) who, in spite of the phenomenal growth of the city in both population and size, refused to extend streetcar tracks to serve those parts of the city not identified in the company's 1891 charter agreement. No matter how hard the city fathers tried to get the company to expand its service, TRC officials refused to improve conditions. After all, the name of the game was to make as much money as possible. And since the franchise had only eleven more years to run that money had to be made now.

To show their displeasure with the TRC's arrogance, civic officials placed the question "are you in favour of the city of Toronto applying to the Legislature for power to construct and operate a municipal system of subway and surface street railways?" on the 1910 municipal election ballot. An equally unhappy electorate gave its approval. However, the matter was shelved when Mayor Geary and his new council found themselves confronted with more serious problems.

As the months went by transit service continued to deteriorate and in

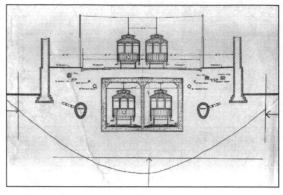

Engineering drawing of the 1912 Toronto subway proposal that would have seen regular streetcars running in tunnels under Yonge Street.

1912, championed by aldermanic candidate Horatio Hocken, a plan to build a subway was again placed on the municipal election ballot. This time the project was identified more precisely as running from the Bay and Front intersection to Yonge and St. Clair and requiring the expenditure of $5,386,870 out of the taxpayers' collective pockets.

With the civic indebtedness approaching an astronomical (for the time) $40 million the electorate, faced with the possibility of increased taxes (sound familiar?) to pay for the project rejected the proposal 11,130 to 7,697. Once again Toronto's subway hopes were thwarted.

The next time Torontonians heard about a possible subway for their city they, and the rest of the world, were deep in a depression. The 1931 proposal had 3,000 unemployed men digging a twenty-foot ditch down the middle of Yonge Street through which streetcars would run. This plan didn't even make the ballot.

Finally, with the world at war and every available piece of public transit equipment in the city crammed full with war workers, the TTC began developing its own subway plan, a plan that would require the expenditure of $34 million. On election day, 1946, the electorate overwhelmingly approved both Yonge Street and Queen Street subways, *provided that the Dominion government assume one-fifth of the cost.* As it turned out there was no financial aid from Ottawa and only the Yonge line was built at a cost of $66 million, almost twice the original estimate.

GOIN' DOWN THE "TUBE"

March 27, 1994

You know the years are marching by when, while chatting with someone about Toronto's history, you discover that person never knew our city when it didn't boast a subway. However, like many people, not only do I remember a subway-less Toronto, I also remember the arrival of rapid transit (the term for subway in vogue back then) in Toronto. I also remember getting a half-day off school on that Tuesday, March

The omnipresent Mayor Allan Lamport, accompanied by Ontario Premier Leslie Frost, are welcomed to the official opening ceremonies for the new Yonge subway at Davisville Station, March 30, 1954. *(TTC)*

30, 1954, to ride the brand new 4.6 mile (we didn't have that kilometre stuff back then – heck we didn't even have calculators, just slide rules) Yonge line on its first day of operation.

Oh, and you didn't sit (more likely stand) just anywhere in that shiny red train. It was imperative that you pushed your way to the front of the first car where a huge crowd had convened. As the train rocketed from station to station each and every person in that crowd jostled with fellow travellers to get a good look down the track and, south of Davisville station, into the inky blackness of the ... tunnel. The idea was not to become too carried away by it all just in case the operator, cocooned in his little cubicle safely sheltered from the excited masses, requested you to help him drive the train.

It's hard to believe that forty years have passed since that exciting day in our city's history, a day referred to by the usually unruffled members of the print, radio and fledgling television media (local TV in the form of CBLT Channel 9 had been on the air for less than twenty months) as "S-DAY."

While several attempts had been made since the turn of the century to build a "tube" (as subways were called back then, subways were constructed for vehicles

under busy railway tracks), it wasn't until the electorate gave its overwhelming approval during the 1946 municipal election that work could begin in earnest on Toronto's, and Canada's first subway. (The TTC had begun seriously thinking about a subway in 1942 and actually established a Rapid transit Department two years later with W.H. "Pat" Patterson serving as its first engineer.)

Inaugural subway train southbound at Davisville Station. *(TTC)*

As eager as the city was to build that new line the construction turbulence that followed the war's cessation resulted in a severe shortage of steel and other building materials as well as a scarcity of both skilled and unskilled labourers. The federal government stepped in and rationed what little steel was being turned out and it wasn't until September 8, 1949 that workers were finally able to pound the first subway piling into place at the corner of Yonge and Wellington streets with a young Monty Hall hosting the attendant ceremony.

Originally scheduled to go into service sometime in 1952 the Yonge subway finally opened 1,634 days later, March 30, 1954, exactly 40 years ago this coming Wednesday. Official ceremonies were held at Davisville with the first train, jam packed with VIPs, pulling out of the station at 11:50 AM. A few hours later, at precisely 1:30 PM the doors at all twelve stations were thrown open to the general public and Toronto's first subway was in business; adult fares – three tickets/tokens (the latter introduced for turnstile operation) for a quarter or ten cents cash.

It was estimated that on that first day more than 200,000 people took the ride from Eglinton to Front covering the distance in a remarkable twelve minutes. And just in case you think that cost overruns are a new phenomenon in this city, when all the bills were in for what had been estimated as a $32,450,000 project nine years earlier, inflation typical of the booming '50s had resulted in that figure more than doubling to $67 million.

HISTORIC TRACK

March 13, 1994

Recently, Toronto City Council gave its approval to the eagerly sought expansion of the Metro Convention Centre on Front Street. This multi-million dollar project will see the construction of about one million square feet of additional exhibit space, meeting rooms, parking, etc., under the sprawling open space due south of the railway tracks on property commonly known as the "railway lands."

As part of the understanding reached between representatives of the Convention Centre and the city the historic CPR roundhouse, located at the south end of the property under development, will be retained in anticipation of its eventual rebirth as a dynamic touchstone of an era when the steam railway was king.

∿

The origin of the city's railway lands can be traced back to the middle of the last century when construction of tracks for the young province's first steam railway, the *Ontario, Simcoe & Huron Railway*, resulted in a dedicated right-of-way across the city's waterfront. The mandate of the *OH&S* was to provide a rail connection between the bustling provincial capital on Lake Ontario and developing communities on the shores of the last two lakes identified in the company's title.

The advantages of the railway over road and water travel (hindered as they were by inclement weather conditions) as a means of transportation for both people and goods to and from the big city soon resulted in the establishment of more railway companies and routes. Invariably these routes resulted in additional tracks being laid along the water's edge occasionally without city approval, frequently without its blessing.

The most serious problem arising from the indiscriminate construction of these rights-of-ways was the barrier they formed between the city proper and its waterfront. Pedestrians and wheeled-vehicles navigating major north-south thoroughfares, like York, Bay and Yonge, were forced to negotiate more than a dozen pairs of tracks. The problem was made even worse by lengthy freight trains straddling the crossings or by huge steam engines shunting back and forth. Occasionally impatient Island-bound pedestrians would attempt to crawl under the cars all too often with fatal results.

Finally, in an effort to alleviate an intolerable situation (and to fit in with the requirements of the new Union Station then nearing completion), plans were formulated to tidy up the tangle of tracks and crossings by elevating the railway lands seventeen feet and constructing a cross-waterfront viaduct under which road subways to and from the wharves and docks were constructed. A new "High Line," by which freight traffic could skirt the southern edge of the railway lands, was also planned.

The Canadian Pacific Railway, which had gained a toe-hold on the railway lands through its acquisition of the Credit Valley Railway in 1883, decided to modernize its John Street Coach Yard and replace the existing 1893 roundhouse.

Work on a new concrete, brick and wood roundhouse, to a design produced by CPR's Engineering Department, commenced in 1929 and a year later all but the extreme west end of the huge new facility had been completed. In 1930 the older, smaller roundhouse, which had continued in service while the new structure was being erected, was demolished and the site cleared. On part of this site, four additional stalls were added to the west end of the new facility giving it a total of thirty-two stalls, one of the largest in the nation.

To facilitate engine movements into and out of the new roundhouse, a 120-foot-long, three-point turntable operated by compressed air was constructed. In addition, a 60,000-gallon elevated water tank and 320-ton capacity coaling and sand tower, a coach repair shop (since demolished) and stores building were part of the John Street complex.

CPR's new John Street roundhouse (with twenty-eight of the thirty-two stalls completed), the 120-foot turntable foundation, coaling tower and stores building are seen under construction in this 1929 photo. Part of the 1893 roundhouse, where four more stalls would be erected, can be seen to the extreme right. Elevation of the entire property (a total of seventeen feet using thousands of cubic yards of landfill material) is also apparent (bottom right). In the background we see the newly completed two-million-bushel grain elevator of Toronto Elevators Limited (which was demolished in 1983), harbour reclamation and, over on the Island, the Hanlan's Point baseball/lacrosse stadium.

TAKE ME OUT TO
THE OLD BALL GAME

April 3, 1994

As we get set for the opening ball game tomorrow, I wonder how many of the fans at the game will be under the impression that "baseball fever" is a relatively new phenomenon, probably experienced in this city for the very first time by the 44,649 shivering fans at Exhibition Stadium back on that cold April 7, 1977 day when the newborn Jays took to the field for the first time. Wrong! Professional baseball has a longer history than that in this town.

Much longer in fact. Why, some of the more senior fans in tomorrow's SkyDome crowd may be able to recall an earlier wave of "baseball fever" that hit the city each time the Maple Leafs of the International League started a new season at Fleet Street Flats, an ultra modern ball yard located at the southwest corner of Lake Shore Boulevard (known until 1960 as Fleet Street) and Bathurst.

And then there are the more senior seniors (and boy would I like to chat with them) that may even remember the hoopla attendant with the season openers that thrilled fans even before Lol Solman's place on reclaimed land at the foot of Bathurst came into existence in 1926.

From 1897 until 1925 pro baseball attracted thousands to Hanlan's Point over on the Island. In fact, so popular was the sport at the turn of the century for while a total of twelve ferryboats shuttled back and forth across the bay desperately trying to keep up with the boisterous crowds seeking to take in the game.

And while it's quite likely there's no one around today (more's the pity) who remembers the game being played in Toronto earlier than 1897, the newspapers as far back as 1885 carried graphic accounts of the "boys of summer" playing their hearts out at rudimentary baseball diamonds at the northwest corner of Jarvis and Wellesley streets, at the Rosedale lacrosse field or at the Toronto Baseball Grounds tucked away at the southwest corner of Queen and Broadview.

Take, for instance, the following report that appeared in the May 14, 1888 edition of *The Evening Telegram* describing the previous Saturday's game between teams representing Toronto and London, Ontario. in the International Association, forerunner of the International League. I've reproduced the article verbatim so that none of the style and enthusiasm of a reporter covering baseball in our city more than a century ago, and identified only as *The Khan,* is lost.

First Blue Jay ball game ... in the snow! April 7, 1977.
(Photo by Norm Betts, Toronto Sun)

A southerly wind and a cloudy sky proclaimed it a baseball afternoon. The scene on the streets also proclaimed the fact that this world is veritably up and down and no mistake for preceded by tuneful bands there rolled carriage after carriage full of sunburned and uniformed young gentlemen some of whom were not very long ago coal heavers in Pennsylvania, log rustlers in Michigan or "run wid de gang in Brooklyn." But now, because "dey can tro' der ball" behold them lolling in carriages much as home as my lords who were accustomed to carriages from their infancy. But, perhaps in a few weeks from now some of them, after making a few costly errors, will be relegated to the opposition benches and will be painfully enquiring "Mister, can you give me a job?." Yes, for the time being, each and every one of them was an object of sincere admiration and they were studied and examined as curiously as if they were scions of the reigning house. The Tecumsehs *of London were to play the* Torontos *the first league game of the season on the latter's own ground. So from two until half past three a steady stream of humanity poured across the Don to view a rather rocky exhibition of the great national game of our neighbours across the line. There were thousands on thousands there rushing and squeezing against each other 'til the grounds and the grandstands presented a scene that had to be witnessed to be appreciated. The people of Alexandria and Rome in days gone by filled vast amphitheaters to their fullest seating capacity in order to witness chariot race, gladiatorial combats and the awful struggles of strong men against savage wild beasts, but is questionable if they ever showed as much delight as did the Toronto audience on Saturday when Mr. Atkisson* (pitcher Albert Atkisson, 33 wins in 1888) *the "twirler" the obnoxious fat second baseman of the Tecumsehs or exhibited as much horror and dismay as did that Saturday audience when the men from the wooly west got a run in the first inning. When the tiger from the Colliseum suddenly bounded from his cage and rushed panting at the gladiator in the middle of the arena the 20,000 Romans never held their breath tighter than did the 5,000 Torontonians on Saturday when Mr. Decker* (Harry Decker, batting avr.313) leaped from the bag at first base and started out like a fiery, untamed stead to "steal" second. And when the brave adventurer got there safely sat on the bag and dusted his knees and was declared safe.

> Toronto sent up a rapturous cry,
> And the London men, with tearful eye,
> Could scarce forbear to cheer.

My heart, hardened by a long winter and late spring, was stirred when the voice-ful 5,000 lifted the roof off with a yell when the fleet-footed Mr. Connor caught a running fly in left field and prevented another run. Yes, mine eyes were filled [with] sympathetic tears as I viewed the anxious and sorrowful faces around when the distinguished Mr. McLaughlin fumbled a "hot one" and let "bad-man-with-the-nimble-hoof" get his base unharmed. But the greatest excitement took place when the gentleman with padded legs and a voice like the bleat of a 2 year-old Holstein in agony – the umpire – made a close decision. Then did the players flock around that unhappy little man while the indignant 5,000, who held that Mr. Rickley was perfectly and unquestionably "safe" filled the circumambient air with groans that addled the sparrows under the eaves. Another party who was very conspicuous is Mr. Cushman (manager Charles Cushman, winning average .607), who like Frederick William, Mr. Chamberlain and other celebrities has been spoken much of late. He pranced up and down in front of the grandstand, threatened the restless boy with a Bismarkian air and tried to look perfectly unconcerned when an admirer pointed him out to a friend and said, perhaps too audibly, "that's him." Mr. Cushman has got to be a big boy now since he stood behind the front dash board of a bob-tailed car (horse-drawn streetcar) in Philadelphia guiding it through that city's principal streets. He "fares" better now than he did then.

It was a great afternoon's sport. There were some great plays and some very bad ones. It was painful to see Mr. Power's agriculturalists cantering after a ball like a man trying to head off a pig – it was really. The Torontos played gracefully, but they were playing against an inferior team – it was Paul Pattillo against Polly Wants-a-cracker. But everybody enjoyed themselves. The gentlemen stamped and cheered or groaned and hissed and the little fellow with the padded shins. The ladies – and there were many of them – waved their handkerchiefs, the small boys shrieked. Mr. Cushman walked to and fro like a silent man of destiny and the little German band made a few selections forever unpopular in this neighbourhood.

And now a word to the management. The sooner the rowdyism which disgraced the close of Saturday's game is put a stop to the better for the credit of baseball. A nod is as good as a wink to a blind horse.

And so a really pleasant afternoon came to a close. Toronto won the vast and good humoured multitude poured forth the victors and the vanquished rolled through them and the small boy stopped you on the street corner to enquire "who won, mister?"

SUPER SERVICE

April 10, 1994

I was the after-dinner speaker at a life insurance convention the other evening and following my presentation spent some time chatting with a few "senior" Torontonians about the good old days. The topic eventually turned to their collective memories of the long-gone gasoline stations that use to be found on practically every other street corner.

Some of the names they reflected on included Red Indian, White Rose, Crown Dominion, Lion, British America, Cities Service, Perfection, Supreme, Imperial, Shell and Sun (of course, those last three are still with us, Sun as Sunoco). Suddenly someone mentioned a name that instantly took me back to my high school days at North Toronto Collegiate when, to make a little pocket money and/or a few gallons of gas for my

A typical early 1930s Supertest ad drawn by cartoonist Jimmy "Birdseye centre" Frise.
(Courtesy B.J. Moser, Petro Canada)

'58 Hillman Minx (with its broken ring gear). I helped out at Harry Norman's gas station at the southwest corner of Mt. Pleasant Road and Belsize Drive.

Harry had moved to the Belsize corner after many years in partnership with Jan Wietzes, running a gas station/Rootes dealership just around the corner from where I lived on Elvina Gardens. It was Harry who sold me that Hillman though I really lusted after a red Sunbeam Alpine. (Wouldn't you know it ... by the time I could afford an Alpine, they'd stopped making them.)

After Harry moved down the street to run a BP station, Jan and his boys, Bert and Eppie, moved to north Yonge and opened a Toyota dealership where I wound up buying a succession of Celicas.

Oh, I almost forgot. The name of that brand of gasoline that got me started on this trip down my own personal memory lane, a brand that used to be as familiar as today's Esso and Shell ... Supertest.

Supertest stations, and the Supertest brand of gasoline, were the creation of John Gordon Thompson, a one-time traveling salesman who was born in Aylmer, Ontario exactly one century ago.

After a stint overseas during the Great War with Canadian Army's Service Corps and two years as an industrial survey officer for the Soldiers' Civil Re-establishment Commission, Thompson opened a small tire shop in London, Ontario, that two years later he converted into the country's first vulcanizing plant.

As a sideline he began manufacturing gasoline pumps, the type with the tall, graduated glass container on top into which the gasoline was pumped using a hand lever and then allowed to flow into the car or truck gas tank by gravity.

On day, while traveling on business in the States, Thompson pulled into a small gasoline station adjacent to a general store to gas up. He was amazed when the friendly attendant asked if the traveler would like his car's windshield and rear view mirror cleaned. In all the years that Thompson had driven in his home province, the idea of getting anything more than a tank of gasoline at a gas pump was unheard of. His experience with this friendly and helpful

Harry Norman and Jan Wietzes operated a Supertest station on Fleet Street (now Lake Shore Blvd. West) from 1953 until 1958. The fellows moved to a new location at Mt. Pleasant Road and Broadway which they ran, with help from Jan's sons Eppie and Bert, until November 1965. It was here that I purchased my first car. Since December 1965, the two boys have operated Wietzes Motors Ltd. on north Yonge Street in Willowdale. *(Courtesy Bert Wietzes)*

gas jockey stayed with Thompson and when he returned to London he decided that Ontario motorists would take their business to a station where, in addition to gasoline (which they could get anywhere) they could also get extra assistance. Staff at his stations would provide that extra assistance by cleaning the car windshield and lights and checking the radiator, engine oil and tire pressure. And that extra service would be provided not only in a friendly manner, but for free!

And so it was that in 1923 Thompson started his own gasoline company under the name Supertest. He established a "courtesy school" for all his attendants. Before long he operated stations not just in London, but in Ottawa, Montreal and Toronto as well. By the mid-1940s there were thirty-nine Supertest stations in Toronto alone.

In 1973, the Supertest name vanished forever when Thompson's company was acquired by BP (a company that itself had a history going back to 1908 – as Anglo-Persian Petroleum – and which had purchased the Canadian Cities Service business in 1962). In 1983, one year after multi-millionaire J. Gordon Thompson passed away, BP in turn was purchased by Petro Canada, a company established in 1975.

Ultra modern Petro Canada station. *(Courtesy B.J. Moser, Petro Canada)*

HAPPY BIRTHDAY TO TORONTO ISLAND

April 17, 1994

Hands up those of you who wished our very own Toronto Island a "Happy Birthday" last Wednesday? You forgot? Shame!

Well, perhaps that forgetfulness is excusable. After all, it has been a long time since the present chain of more than a dozen islands, some large, some small, enclosing the south side of Toronto Bay came into being. One hundred and thirty-six years to be exact.

Watching the ships enter and leave Toronto Harbour via the East Gap, as in this turn-of-the-century snapshot, became a popular summer pastime.

History tells us that it was on April 13, 1858, that The Peninsula, as the land enclosing the south side of Toronto Harbour had been referred to by the pioneer settlers, officially lost that precise geographical characterization.

On that day, an unusually heavy rainfall caused watercourses in and around the young city to overflow their banks inundating Toronto's dusty streets and laneways and causing minor panic amongst the community's 48,000 or so inhabitants. The downpour was so intense that the outflow from the Don River caused the narrow isthmus connecting The Peninsula with the mainland due south of the river's outlet (see map) to be breached thereby creating the present island formation. In the process a small hotel imprudently erected right on the narrow land bridge was washed away. Over the ensuing years, that breach has been widened, stabilized and reinforced and is now referred to as the East Gap.

Though the conversion of The Peninsula into a true island didn't finally come to pass until the spring of 1858, the idea of a permanent eastern entrance to the harbour had been advocated by citizens for many years. With the vast majority of sailing ships calling at the Port of Toronto approaching the city from the east, much time was lost as these craft carefully made their way around the south side of The Peninsula making for the West Gap. On several occasions sudden deterioration of the weather resulted in serious accidents often with the loss of both cargo and life.

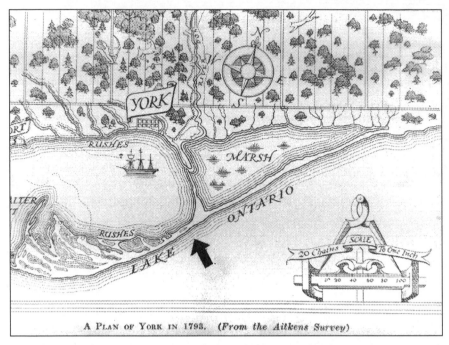

A PLAN OF YORK IN 1793. *(From the Aitkens Survey)*

Early map of York (now Toronto) showing the narrow isthmus (arrow) that connected *The Peninsula* with the mainland until its removal following a severe rain storm 136 years ago.

As early as 1835, just one year after the City of Toronto came into being, several influential businessmen met at one of the young city's pioneer hotels to discuss how they might convince the government to construct a new eastern entrance to the harbour.

A committee was finally appointed to look into the pros and cons of constructing a new entrance. While nothing came of this particular committee's efforts, unofficial talks continued with some suggesting that without a new entrance the harbour would soon become a stagnant, putrid body of water. Others, including the well respected harbourmaster Hugh Richardson, said that a new eastern entrance would hasten the destruction of the already deteriorating western entrance.

In the meantime, Mother Nature was also getting involved. Violent storms in 1853, 1856 and 1857 resulted in huge waves washing away large portions of the narrow isthmus. Each time, city officials would try to fill the breach with pine posts and sand leaving a very unstable land bridge with the mainland. Finally, the rain storm that ravaged the city 136 years ago last Wednesday did the trick and Toronto Island was born.

CONNECT ME WITH ...

April 24, 1994

S o these two guys were chatting. One asked the other if he'd had a chance to look through the new telephone book? "Nah," said the other. "You should," his friend shot back. "The plot may be lousy, but it sure has a great list of characters."

Well, one of Bell Canada's new phone books recently arrived on my doorstep. Bell's friendly PR people tell me that this edition of the directory contains exactly 1,090,593 entries in the white pages with an additional 10,431 listings in the government blue section. More than 4,700 tons of paper, 68 tons of ink and 25 tons of glue were used to put together the April 1994–1995 Metro Toronto phone book.

My guess is that it won't be long before this five-pound tome will be replaced by one of those computer mini-discs like the one on which I store my *Sun*

When the new automatic, or machine-switching system was introduced in the summer of 1924 (the Grover exchange was first), it became necessary for Bell Telephone officials to provide instructions on how to use this new technology. In this photo from the Bell Canada Telephone Historical Collection bobby-helmeted Toronto policemen are tutored on the art of using the new "dial" telephone. *(CTA)*

columns. Just slip the disc into the slot on the old "386" (can't afford a "486"), enter a name and, presto, the address, perhaps complete with postal code imported from another data disc, and phone number will flashed on the screen.

The new Metro phone directory is sure a far cry from the city's first so-called "phone book," a diminutive manual that was issued by the Toronto Telephone Despatch Company exactly 115 years ago this year.

Released in April of 1879 this pioneer directory was really just a printed list of the forty Torontonians who had subscribed to the company's revolutionary new communications service using Alexander Graham Bell's new invention, the telephone.

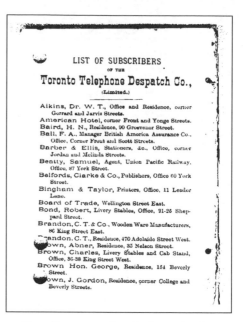

LIST OF SUBSCRIBERS
OF THE
Toronto Telephone Despatch Co.,
(Limited.)

Aikins, Dr. W. T., Office and Residence, corner Gerrard and Jarvis Streets.
American Hotel, corner Front and Yonge Streets.
Baird, H. N., Residence, 90 Grosvenor Street.
Ball, F. A., Manager British America Assurance Co., Office, Corner Front and Scott Streets.
Barber & Ellis, Stationers, &c., Office, corner Jordan and Melinda Streets.
Beatty, Samuel, Agent, Union Pacific Railway, Office, 87 York Street.
Belfords, Clarke & Co., Publishers, Office 60 York Street.
Bingham & Taylor, Printers, Office, 11 Leader Lane.
Board of Trade, Wellington Street East.
Bond, Robert, Livery Stables, Office, 21-25 Sheppard Street.
Brandon, C. T. & Co., Wooden Ware Manufacturers, 86 King Street East.
Brandon, C. T., Residence, 470 Adelaide Street West.
Brown, Abner, Residence, 35 Nelson Street.
Brown, Charles, Livery Stables and Cab Stand, Office, 36-38 King Street West.
Brown Hon. George, Residence, 154 Beverly Street.
Brown, J. Gordon, Residence, corner College and Beverly Streets.

Page from an early telephone book.

To exploit Bell's creation, a quartette of prominent city businessmen incorporated The Toronto Telephone Despatch Company in 1878, just four years after Bell began working on his invention in Brantford, Ontario, and two years after he uttered his famous statement "Watson come here, I want you" in his Boston, Massachusetts laboratory.

Represented on that list were the company shareholders (brothers Abner and Melvin Rosebrugh, Charles Potter and Hugh Neilson), four city doctors, three druggists, two newspapers, one telegraph company, one optician and one restaurant. Also listed were the provincial premier, the Hon. Oliver Mowat, the Board of Trade office on Wellington Street East, Robert Walker and Sons' dry goods shop on King and several other businesses and residents.

The names were not listed alphabetically nor were the subscribers issued actual phone numbers. It was simply a matter of ringing the "Central Office" (located in a 12' X 12' foot square office on the second floor of the building 10 King Street East) and asking the operator (who was on duty 24 hours a day) to be connected with the subscriber on that list of 40 with whom you wished to converse. As soon as the connection was made, the operator would announce to both parties "all right" and the conversation could begin.

As speaking and listening were done via the same instrument, it was impossible to hold a two-way conversation. One party would have to speak, holding the apparatus in front of the mouth, then move it to the ear to listen for the reply. The other person would reverse this procedure listening first, then speak. As a notice in the directory advised, "Give your hearers ample time to transfer the telephone to their ear before you speak and be certain a sentence is finished before you reply." Simultaneous conversation on the infant telephone wasn't possible back then.

It wasn't long after the company's first directory appeared that more and more Torontonians began to see the advantage of Bell's new communications device (to use modern phraseology). When the fall, 1879 directory appeared the number of subscribers had nearly quadrupled to 150. Three years later there were 400. In 1926, a half-century after Bell's historic directive to his assistant, there were 155,000 phones in Toronto, one for every $3^1/_2$people on that year's assessment role.

SCHOOL DAYS

May 1, 1994

This year is special for one of East York's oldest schools. William Burgess School, which was originally known as Torrens Avenue School after the dirt pathway on which it fronted, a pathway that served to separate several nearby market gardens, was constructed in 1914 at a cost of $100,000, a figure that included the price of the property owned by Mark Maynard, a prominent local contractor.

The name of the new school was changed a few years later to honour William Burgess (1868–1944) who served as a township school trustee for a total of four decades. Burgess lived in a small house that still stands on Logan Avenue near Bee, the latter now renamed Cosburn Avenue. Bob Ogden, the school's vice-principal, is eagerly collecting "Burgess memorabilia" (give him a call at 396-2490 if you have anything) and is authoring a special commemorative book on the history of both the school and neighbourhood that'll be for sale at the school. To help celebrate the school's eight decades of service to the community all former students are invited to drop by the school gym on Wednesday, May 11 between 10:00 AM and 3:00 PM and take part in a day-long get-together. The following evening, Thursday, May 12, former teachers and other staff members will be hosted at a special reception at the school.

Trustee William Burgess, after whom the East York school is named,
and his family. *(Courtesy William Burgess School Archives)*

Neighbours and friends of William Burgess School are invited to drop by during anniversary week May 9th through the 13th. Call the school at 396-2492 for more details.

While on the subject of schools, there's a building at the southeast corner of Bloor and Queen's Park Crescent (just across from the Royal Ontario Museum) that with its Ionic pillars and majestic façade looks more like some palatial residence in England than an educational facility. In fact, the pillars and decorated doorway are reproductions of those found on the Temple of Erechtheum that stands beside the Parthenon in the Acropolis.

Since 1981 this marvelous building has been the Office of the Ombudsman for the province of Ontario though it actually opened sixty-eight years earlier as the Lillian Massey School of Household Sciences and Art. The genesis of this facility goes back exactly a century when industrialist Hart Massey gave his daughter Lillian permission to start a cooking class in the basement of the new Fred Victor Mission on Queen Street East. The mission, which had been named by its benefactor in honour of his recently deceased son, Fred Victor Massey, opened its doors on October 24, 1894, to serve Torontonians in need. It was only fitting that in Lillian's cooking classes those responsible for providing meals for the needy could be taught the fundamentals of preparing nourishing family meals and the essentials of good housekeeping.

Eventually Miss Massey's classes became filled to overflowing with eager "students" and in 1905 the first plans to enlarge the classroom facilities were formulated. A site north of the Queen's Park and adjacent to a tree and residence-lined Bloor Street was selected and on December 3, 1908, the cornerstone of architect George Miller's new building was laid. Five years later, on January 28, 1913, the three-story structure, complete with library, gymnasium, swimming pool, laboratories and fifty classrooms was formally opened by Dr. Robert Falconer, president of the University of Toronto.

The course of instruction offered by the new school included "the study of the scientific principles underlying the care of the utensils and furnishings of a house," "the study of textiles, food and food values" and "instruction in the care and management of the sick room," "the economics of spending, the division of income, the home in its relation to society" and numerous other subjects.

The Lillian Massey School of Household Sciences and Art soon after its official opening in 1913.

CATHEDRAL
THAT MIGHT HAVE BEEN

May 8, 1994

Nestled on a side street not far from the old community of Seaton Village and just a few blocks north of the busy Bloor/Bathurst intersection is a hulking mass of bricks that, had fate been kinder, would have had the distinction of becoming the prestigious cathedral church of the Anglican Diocese of Toronto. But that was not to be. History decreed that St. James' in downtown Toronto would be bestowed with that honour.

One version of the proposed St. Alban's Cathedral, Howland and Barton streets.

ᏉᏉ

History reveals that the present St. James' at King and Church streets stands on the site of the very first church in our city (that structure being the reason for the latter street name). As the congregation of that pioneer wooden house of worship, known simply as "the church at York" (it didn't have a real name until Bishop Stewart of Quebec dedicated it to Saint James the Apostle in 1828), grew in size it became necessary to erect a series of larger, more substantial structures with the present, and fourth to grace the corner, dating back to 1853.

Today, in addition to being a parish church, St. James' is also recognized as a cathedral where the Bishop of Toronto's "cathedra" or chair is located. It has held this honour since 1839 when its rector, John Strachan, was ordained the city's first bishop.

Not satisfied with a mere parish church serving as the diocese cathedral Strachan soon began seeking support for the construction of a new, grander structure that would be built specifically as the Church of England's new cathedral. His plea went unheeded. In fact, it wasn't until 1883, sixteen years after the first bishop's death, that the third Bishop of Toronto, Arthur Sweatman, revived the idea and was successful in having a government Bill passed incorporating the new Cathedral of St. Alban-the-Martyr, so named to honour an officer in the Roman army who converted to Christianity for which he was beheaded near the present St. Albans in Hertfordshire, England, in 304 AD.

In 1885 construction began on the new cathedral designed by architect Richard Windeyer who had based his concept on St. Alban's Abbey in England. By 1891, much of what we see today at the Howland/Barton corner was in place. More than $70,000 had been spent and with a severe business recession hovering over the land and other demands on the rapidly expanding diocese the rest of the massive structure including the 135-foot-high tower would have to wait.

An attempt to raise funds to complete the structure, the design of which had been altered significantly by its new architect R. A. Cram (Windeyer had died in 1900), was started in 1911 under the chairmanship of Sir Henry Pellatt, who had just moved into his new residence, Casa Loma. This attempt was partially successful and only a meager amount of additional work could be done.

Unfortunately for those hoping (and praying) that St. Alban-the-Martyr would eventually become the prestigious cathedral pictured in the architect's sketches, a combination of church politics, a revised construction figure of many hundreds of thousands of dollars and plans to build a new St. Paul's on Bloor Street East all combined to dictate the building's ultimate fate.

All hopes of cathedral status were dashed in 1936 when St. Alban became a simple parish church and some of the four and a half acres of land surrounding the forlorn looking structure was sold for building sites.

Royal St. George's College, a private boy's school established in 1964, took up residence in the former rectory of St. Alban's, just north of the church, made changes to the "cathedral-that-might-have-been" and began using it for various school programs. Royal St. George's is presently discussing the possible purchase of the property surrounding the church.

A somewhat abbreviated St. Alban's as it looks today.

TIME TRACKS

May 15, 1994

There's been lots in the news lately about the creation of new transit routes here in Metro. In fact, not too many weeks ago the media covered in great detail Metro Council's formal approval of the construction of a pair of new subway lines, one under Sheppard Avenue East in North York and another under Eglinton Avenue West in York.

Dozens of nattily attired dignitaries posed for the newspaper photographer's camera in this c. 1893 photo.

When the original Yonge subway opened forty years ago, and again when the Bloor-Danforth opened in 1966 the Toronto papers went so far as to issue special souvenir inserts.

The opening of new transit lines (to use modern-day terminology) has always been newsworthy. This was especially so around the turn of the century when numerous new lines opened as the owners of the street railway companies of the day realized they could make a bundle by providing access to and from the numerous small communities that were blossoming around a growing Toronto.

The Toronto & Mimico Electric Light and Power Company, a privately owned enterprise that began operating a street railway line between Sunnyside and the Humber River in the summer of 1892, was a prime example of this entrepreneurship. The T & M had on its board of directors the well-known boatbuilder and contractor, Octavius Hicks, who lived in a house/boatbuilding factory near the eastern terminus of the street railway line.

Hicks was not only a director, but also laid the line's tracks along a dusty Lake Shore Road, built bridges over the Humber River and (as the line was extended westerly to Salisbury Avenue, now Park Lawn Road, through Long Branch and on to Port Credit in 1905) over the Mimico and Etobicoke Creeks. He also constructed the company's powerhouse at the Humber and was in charge of the day-to-day operation of the line.

Service, on what quickly became a popular summer attraction, was provided by a pair of unique St. Catharines-built double-deck streetcars that were powered by electric motors manufactured in Waterford, Ontario. Unfortunately, these quaint vehicles were unreliable and when spare motor parts couldn't be obtained, more modern utilitarian vehicles were introduced.

In 1893, the Toronto & Mimico came under the control of the privately owned Toronto Railway Company that operated, amongst a myriad of other lines, the entire Toronto city system. In the early 1920s the newly organized and municipally controlled Toronto Transportation Commission took over the Lake Shore route.

Although the Long Branch–Port Credit stretch was abandoned in 1935, the TTC continues to provide service along this pioneer street railway route introducing its modern new CLRV cars to the streetcar traveling public on the 507 Long Branch line in 1979.

News of "the war to end all wars" filled the papers on October 10, 1914, yet room was still found to cover the opening of another interesting commuter line. The Woodbridge Extension of the Toronto Suburban Railway Company's (TSR) Weston route provided passenger and freight service between Keele and Dundas streets in the Junction via Thistletown to Stop 36, Pine Street in the village of Woodbridge twelve miles to the north. This line opened just two months after the Great Depression erupted and was abandoned nearly a dozen years later.

From 1916 to 1931, the TSR also operated a high-speed electric commuter line to Guelph via Cooksville, Streetsville, Georgetown and Acton. The Halton County Radial Railway near Rockwood, Ontario, now operates a collection of vintage streetcars on a portion of this line's right-of-way.

The first radial car into Woodbridge was photographed for the October 10, 1914 edition of the *Evening Telegram*. Standing at the left of the photo is Col. George Royce (Royce Avenue, now Dupont Street), general manager of the TSR.

MOMENTS TO REMEMBER

May 22, 1994

The other day, while listening to Jim Paulson "spin the platters" on CHWO AM1250, the Oakville "oldies" radio station, I heard a song that "topped the charts" for weeks back in 1956. It suddenly occurred to me that in this supposedly "enlightened" day and age, a few of the lyrics in that song could be interpreted by some as being totally sexist. The words:

Standing on the corner,
Watching all the girls go by,
Standing on the corner,
Giving all the girls the eye,
Brother you can't go to jail for what your thinking,
Or for the woo look in your eyes,
You're only standing on the corner,
Watching all the girls go by.

I'm kidding of course. Actually, what really brought the memories flooding back was when Jim talked a bit about the group that made *Standing on the Corner* such a big hit, Toronto's own Four Lads, and the fact that one of them, baritone Frank Busseri, is keeping the group's name alive with a modern version of the Four Lads who perform at various venues in both Canada and the States. I recently chatted with Frank at his Oakville residence.

Toronto teenagers Connie Codarini, Bernie Toorish, Jimmy Arnold and Frank Busseri first met in 1948 while singing in the Bond Street classrooms of St. Michael's Cathedral Choir School. Frequently, after performing the mandatory Gregorian chants, scales and traditional spirituals with fellow classmates, the boys would get together on their own to work on a repertory that included old-time barbershop tunes and up-beat pop numbers. The boys gained valuable experience performing at weddings, dances and the occasional store opening. And even though they were good enough to land a booking at a local hotel, Ontario's strict liquor laws of the day prevented the boys from appearing.

Nevertheless, The Jordanaires, The Otnorots (Toronto backwards) or The Four Dukes (the group's name was as variable as the venue) managed to get an appearance on the popular "Arthur Godfrey Talent Scouts" show where, using the latter name, the boys came in a respectable second.

However, a long distance call to the broadcasting studio after the show advised in no uncertain terms that there was already a group in Detroit using the name The Four Dukes, "so ya better change it, see."

In April of 1950, a chance to perform at New York City's Le Ruban Bleu nitery came the still nameless group's way. Now they had to have a name, or to paraphrase the Le Ruban Bleu's legendary impresario Julius Monk, "you 4 lads need a new name." And there it was. Now as The Four Lads the four Toronto boys were ready to make music history.

So successful was the group's stint at the New York restaurant that the two-week contract was extended to thirty. *Variety* magazine caught the act and in the May 24, 1950 issue reviewed the act in these words:

There's a youthful earnestness about them. .. sing in French and English and have a catalog that includes novelty tunes, ballads and an occasional spiritual ... they should do well in cafés, theatres and videos (the latter term referring to motion pictures and obviously not today's music videos). Note that the term *recordings* was not included.

At the 1955 CNE Toronto's Four Lads met Toronto's "Lady of the Lake," Marilyn Bell, who in 1954 had become the first person to swim Lake Ontario. The boys were featured at the afternoon grandstand show.
(Courtesy Marilyn Bell DiLascio)

An audition with Mitch Miller of Columbia Records resulted in the boys providing background voices for up-and-coming superstar Johnnie Ray's first recording *Whiskey and Gin*. The boys were also heard on Ray's two-sided smash hit record, *Cry* and *The Little White Cloud that Cried*, that sold more than two million copies in just six months! "The Prince of Wails," as Ray was nicknamed, became the most popular celebrity to ever appear at Toronto's Casino Theatre that stood on Queen Street where the Sheraton Centre's main entrance is now located. The Four Lads were also heard on recordings by Doris Day, Jill Corey, Tony Arden and Frankie Laine.

In the spring of 1952, the boys released their first solo recording, *Mocking Bird* (which was reissued again in 1956 and in stereo [!] in 1958), followed by *Istanbul (Not Constantinople)*, *Skokiaan* and *Gilly, Gilly Ossenfetter By the Sea* (who says the songs of today are weird). Then on June 21, 1955, they recorded their biggest hit ever, *Moments to Remember*, selling more than four million copies while riding the charts for a remarkable twenty-six weeks. That song quickly became the group's signature tune.

Other hits for The Four Lads included *No, Not Much* and *Standing on the Corner* (both 1956), *Put a Light in the Window* (1957) and their last record for Columbia *Happy Anniversary* (1959).

Today, Jimmy teaches music in Sacramento, California, Connie runs a restaurant in Cleveland, Ohio, Bernie sells insurance, also in Cleveland, while Frank, as mentioned, continues to stay busy in the music business.

LAID TO REST BY DESIGN

May 29, 1994

Marion Martin, first person buried in
Mt. Pleasant Cemetery.

One of the prettiest "parks" in Metro isn't a park at all. It's a cemetery, Mt. Pleasant Cemetery in fact. Unlike many other burying grounds Mt. Pleasant was designed from the very beginning with a new concept for cemeteries in mind. Its owner, the trustees of the Toronto General Burying Grounds, decided their new suburban cemetery up Yonge Street north of the Third Concession road (now St. Clair Avenue) in the small community of Deer Park would be a "landscape cemetery" in many ways similar to Mt. Auburn Cemetery in Cambridge, Massachusetts. Dedicated in 1831, Mt. Auburn, in turn, included features found in various English country gardens and Père Lachaise Cemetery on the outskirts of Paris, France.

Although a new concept in cemetery design, Mt. Pleasant would in fact be the third administered by the Toronto General Burying Grounds trustees. These trustees were well-known Torontonians who, having sincere concerns about the lack of proper burial facilities in the fast-growing city, established a non-profit trust to alleviate what was becoming a serious municipal problem.

The first, known as the Strangers' Burial Ground or, more commonly, Potters' Field and located at the northwest corner of what today is the busy Yonge-Bloor intersection. It was here that non-Catholics and non-Anglicans (they had their own consecrated grounds), those with no religious beliefs and the destitute were laid to rest. Potters' Field accepted its first "resident" in 1826 and by the mid-1850s more than 6,000 souls reposed within the cemetery's six acres that had set the trustees back a staggering (for the time) $300.

As this burial ground began to fill (and as the Village of Yorkville began to expand) a new site was deemed a necessity and in 1855, a private fifteen-acre cemetery overlooking the Don River north of Gerrard Street was acquired with the trustees having to lend the cash-strapped trust $15,000 of the $16,000 purchase price. On July 11, 1855, the Necropolis on Winchester Street became the trust's second cemetery. Eventually, many of the Potters' Field "residents" would be reinterred in the Necropolis as the trustees moved to comply with a government decree to shut down the Yonge and Bloor property in the face of rapid development nearby.

Over the years the city continued to grow and, as happens, its citizens continued to pass away. As a result, in 1873 the trustees again decided to acquire a new site only this time the location would be somewhere out in the surrounding countryside so that it wouldn't be overrun by an ever-expanding city, at least not for many, many decades. The site selected was a 200-acre farm

Prussian-born Henry Engelhardt became a landscape gardener after moving to the United States in 1851. He came to Ontario twenty years later and in 1875 was hired to lay out the new Mt. Pleasant Cemetery. Engelhardt died in obscurity in a rented downtown flop-house in 1897. His grave in Mt. Pleasant was recently plaqued by the cemetery administrators.

located on the east side of Yonge Street in York Township. The property stretched easterly one and a quarter miles (one concession in surveyor's terminology) and abutted the 1st Concession Road East or the East York Road (now Bayview Avenue). Work quickly began on developing the new landscape-style of cemetery that was quickly gaining favour in both Europe and in the States. German-born landscape designer Henry Engelhardt was hired to do the initial planning and development (Engelhardt was buried in "his" cemetery following his rather sad demise in a rented room in a poor part of town in 1897). The first burial in the new Mt. Pleasant Cemetery was that of Marion Martin and occurred on March 13, 1876.

On Sunday, June 5, 1994, I will, along with staff of what is now known as Commemorative Services of Ontario, host a walking tour of Mt. Pleasant Cemetery with special emphasis on the majestic Darling and Pearson-designed Mausoleum the first phase of which opened in 1920. We'll meet at 2 PM at the Yonge Street gate, rain or shine.

We'll also "meet" Captain Fluke, a favourite of mine who reposes in his own mausoleum that invariably has a basket of flowers offered by an anonymous donor by the front door. Thanks to Captain James Fluke's great grandson Walter Fluke I have acquired some interesting details about the captain that we'll discuss on the walk. Also on our tour will be the exalted Massey Mausoleum. In addition to the family patriarch Hart Massey, who gave his adopted city several proud buildings and institutions in memory of members of his family, ten other Masseys repose in the mausoleum including Charles Albert in whose memory Massey Music Hall was built by his grieving father. Massey Hall opened exactly 100 years ago this coming June 14 and a special party is planned for June 12. Watch for details.

Aerial view (note biplane wing) of the cemetery c. 1920.

ON THE HOME FRONT

June 5, 1994

Fifty years ago today, the front page of the Monday, June 5, 1944 *Evening Telegram* was blanketed with war stories virtually all of which described the situation in Italy. The paper's headline trumpeted "ALLIES CROSS THE TIBER, PURSUIT NORTH OF ROME." The fight to liberate Italy was well underway. Across the page, in a story headed "Mussolini's Great Sorrow Doesn't Bother Germans," Axis' propaganda writers were attempting to convince their countrymen that the loss of Rome was actually a good thing for Germany because now the need to supply its one million inhabitants plus an additional 30,000 to 40,000 refugees within the city's boundaries, was now a problem for the Allies.

Actually, except for a modest story under the heading "Allied Air Blitz Goes On, Coast Hit Around Clock," page one was almost entirely devoted to the war in Italy. Front page attention to events in the Italian theatre of war would all but vanish in the June 6 edition.

∾

In the more than fifty months that had passed since the outbreak of the Second World War Torontonians had become used to scrutinizing the dreaded "casualty lists" in the daily papers and reading heavily censored stories identified simply as having been prepared "With the Allies Somewhere on the Front Line."

But while battles raged in Europe and the Far East, life went on in Ontario's capital city. The entertainment page of the June 5 *Evening Telegram* was full of ads for places where the war could be forgotten if only for a little while.

For instance, the Hotel Embassy on Bloor at Belair ("air-cooled for your comfort") was presenting well-known band leader Ferdy Mowry's Music with songs by Juliette (the Juliette?) and Paul Ross every evening ("cover charge: 75¢ weekdays, $1 Saturdays"). Of course, in 1944, never on Sundays.

A group known as The Century Boys were offering both modern and old-time dancing at the Parkdale Assembly, 10 Lansdowne Avenue ("corner Queen") while over at Toronto's castle-on-the-hill, Ellis McLintock and the Casa Loma Orchestra were scheduled to play on Wednesday, Friday and Saturday.

There was to be a Promenade Symphony Concert at Varsity Arena on Thursday, June 8 (tickets: reserved 80¢ and 50¢, 1,000 general admission seats, each 25¢), and on Friday evening the pupils of Beth Weyms would give a dance recital in the Jarvis Collegiate Auditorium.

Live theatre that week included, at the good old Royal Alexandra, Melville Cooper and Fritzi Scheff, starring in the "gay comedy & Frederick Lonsdale's

180

best" something called *Aren't We All?* (tickets: 50¢, 75¢, $1 and $1.50 all plus tax).

The movie houses around town were "waving the flag" with *The Fighting Seabees* and *Rosie the Riveter* at the Midtown (Bloor east of Bathurst), *Spitfire* at the KUM-C (1286 Queen Street West) and Beaver (2942 Dundas Street West), *Action in the North Atlantic* at the Mayfair (347 Jane Street) and *Corvette K225* (complete with a brief view of minesweepers being built in Toronto Harbour at the foot of Spadina Avenue) at the Scarboro 958 Kingston Road).

Prior to the American landing at Omaha Beach on D-Day minesweepers of the Royal Canadian Navy, two of which were built by Toronto's Dufferin Shipbuilding Company at the foot of Spadina Avenue (HMCS *Georgian* and HMCS *Thunder*), swept the approaches. In this Toronto Harbour Commission photo HMS *Myrmidon*, one of forty-six minesweepers built for the Royal Navy in Toronto and similar to Toronto's D-Day minesweepers, is launched on October 21, 1944, at the Spadina shipyard. Note the grain elevator (still standing) and lights of old Maple Leaf Stadium (demolished 1968). *(THC)*

∾

That rather matter-of-fact story in the June 5 *Tely* describing the Allied air blitz of the French coast during which British and American aircraft had dropped thousands of tons of explosives on Germany's West Wall fortifications grew in the June 6 edition to fill pages and pages with news of the Allied invasion of Europe. And 15,000 Canadians, including men of Toronto's illustrious Queen's Own Rifles, airmen of the RCAF's 6 Group and officers and ratings of the RCN were in the thick of it! The long anticipated D-Day had arrived.

And when it was over, 359 Canadians had been killed, 584 lay wounded and 131 taken as prisoners-of-war.

But the tide had turned. Less than a year later the world was rid of both Adolph Hitler and his so-called "1,000 year Reich" and soon the world would be at peace.

DIGGING UP TUNNEL TALK

June 12, 1994

So the British and French finally got their long sought-after tunnel. Big deal. Here in Toronto, we nearly got our own tunnel, though I must admit the Toronto project wouldn't have been nearly as long or as expensive. After all, Toronto Island isn't that far away. Nevertheless, both projects have interesting histories.

The new English Channel tunnel, or Chunnel as it's euphemistically called, was first talked about as early as 1802 by Napoleon who would build it after defeating England. Oops!

As the years went by plans for a tunnel connecting Britain with the mainland kept being dug up. Finally, in 1880, construction work actually commenced with workers on both sides of the Channel hard at work. This activity continued for almost four years until suddenly, English attitudes towards the project changed (thanks, some historians claim, to the numerous and powerful British shipping interests who finally had their collective say in the matter). The project came to an end when a brochure appeared describing a fictitious invasion of England via the new tunnel. "Dover Garrison Butchered" screamed one headline, "London Taken, England Conquered" read another. Prime Minister Gladstone was forced to end his country's participation and although the French crews carried on for a time, they too eventually went home.

Since then at least twenty-five attempts have been made to build the elusive tunnel including one in 1931 that came with seven votes of getting official government approval. Another by the Channel Tunnel Company in the mid-1960s would have seen the thirty-three-mile (twenty-three under water, ten under land), $500 million link completed by the end of that decade. The crossing fee was to be pegged at twenty dollars per car (including the driver and two passengers). That one was halted for economic reasons.

Finally, 185 years after Napoleon's grand scheme to invade Britain without his troops becoming seasick, work finally started on a project that would succeed. Then, exactly three years later, English and French workers shook hands under the Channel. Test runs have commenced and soon shuttle trains made up of conventionally passenger cars and Canadian-designed double- and single-deck car and bus transports will zip through the *Chunnel* in regular service.

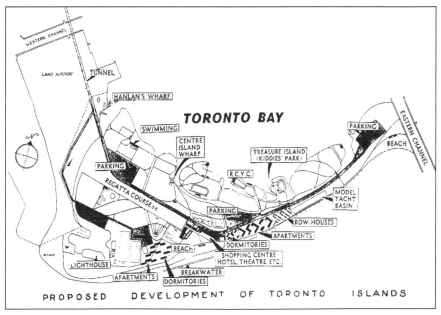

Plans for Toronto's Gunnel (that's a tunnel under the Gap at the west end of Toronto Bay) were put forward in early 1909 when city Parks Commissioner Wilson released his plan to beautify the Island incorporating in that plan a sixteen-foot-wide automobile and pedestrian tunnel under the Gap connecting the "sandbar" with the mainland. Nothing happened. The tunnel got another kick in 1913 when the federal government agreed to build a pair of bridges over the East and West Gaps to serve a new boulevard drive that was to encircle Toronto Island, the drive being part of Wilson's 1909 plan. This plan was confirmed by "Order-in-Council P.C. 1426." It soon became evident that because numerous freighters and passenger ships used those channels the bridge idea would have to be replaced by the tunnel concept. Nothing happened until the mid-1930s when under a plan to put those unemployed because of the deepening Depression to work on projects involving the construction of a trans-Canada highway, improvements to both the St. Lawrence River channel and municipal harbors the federal government under R.B. Bennett awarded a contract to the Dominion Construction Company in the amount of $976,264.

The March 1951 plan for the revitalization of Toronto Island put forward by the city's Board of Control included a long-sought-after tunnel to the mainland. Note that a shopping centre, apartments and a hotel/theatre complex were to be part of the deal.

The company was to construct a 2,200 foot-long tunnel, "with ample provision for streetcars, motor cars and pedestrian traffic," to connect Hanlan's Point on the Western Sandbar with Bathurst Street. To stifle any concerns about the intrusion of vehicles on the car-free Island streetcars would loop at Hanlan's Point while large parking lots would define the terminus of traffic roadbed. Cash-strapped parents would now be able to visit the Island with the whole family without buying extra streetcar tickets for the ferryboat crossing. (The TTC operated the ferries and charged two tickets for the round trip.)

The project came to a crashing halt just seven days after the newly elected Mackenzie King government took office. The pilot tunnel was backfilled and all traces of Toronto's *Gunnel* disappeared.

Over the ensuing years other plans to build the illusive tunnel were put forward including one in 1951 that would also have seen shopping centers, hotels, theaters and apartments erected at Centre Island.

As recently as 1992 City Council endorsed in principle building a "fixed link" (meaning tunnel or bridge) between the Island Airport and the mainland. We'll see.

OUR MASSEY HALL TURNS 100

June 12, 1994

In honour of Massey Hall's centennial, this article appeared in the paper though not as my regular "The Way We Were" column.

When word reached the aging Hart Massey that his eldest son, Charles Albert, had succumbed to the dreaded typhoid fever the family patriarch was devastated. Though he loved his four sons immensely, there was little doubt that Charley was his favorite. And it would be in Charles Albert's memory that Hart would give Toronto and its citizens a marvelous assembly, lecture and music hall. Now, exactly one century after the new hall opened with a grand three-day music festival, Massey Hall continues to be a vital part of the social fabric of our city.

Hart Massey was born on April 29, 1823, on the family farm just north of the small town of Cobourg, Upper Canada, as the Province of Ontario was called in those pre-Confederation days. He attended Cobourg's Victoria College ("Vic" moved to Toronto in 1892) and upon graduation decided to remain at home where he would farm a substantial piece of property given to him by his proud father, Daniel.

As the years went by it became abundantly clear that both father and son were more interested in things mechanical than in the bone wearying day to day running of the two-family farms. In fact, they both saw a brighter future in the development and sale of equipment that would make farm work a little more tolerable. And so it was that in 1847, at the age of forty-nine, Daniel experienced what today we would call a career change and moved his wife, Lucina, and their four youngest children (Hart remained on the farm) to the small community of Newcastle where he opened a small foundry. At first Daniel only built the simplest of farm implements, ploughs and the like, eventually adding a line of cultivators and harrows. Then, using his God-given talents, he began incorporating slight design modifications into his products. Before long implements from Massey's Newcastle Foundry and Machine Manufactory were in short supply, orders far outstripping the small machine shop's capabilities. In 1851 Hart joined his father's business and a year later became a full partner. Business prospered and soon Hart's son Charles Albert was brought into the fold.

Charley, as his father referred to him with great affection, was born on September 20, 1848, and as a child always displayed a talent for things musical. In fact, he could sight-read with ease and from the age of just thirteen was often called on to play the cabinet organ at the local Methodist Church. In later years, while attending his father's alma mater Victoria College in Cobourg he would spend countless hours playing the harmonium in his dormitory room. So great was Charley's love of music that when, on October 12, 1870, he was betrothed to pretty Jessie Arnold, Hart gave the young groom both a harmonium and a piano as wedding gifts. Years later his son's love for music would prompt Hart to memorialize his son's memory with a building that has become a true Toronto landmark.

Music Hall's namesake Charles Albert Massey, 1848–1884.

Massey Music Hall (the "Music" part of the moniker was dropped when the term music hall began to take on a rather bawdy connotation) as it appeared soon after the opening a century ago. The ugly, but necessary, fire escapes, that now mar the façade, were added in 1911.

On the advice of the family doctor a weary Hart Massey turned the day-to-day foundry operations over to Charley and moved with the remainder of the family to Cleveland. There he met Sidney Badgley, a Canadian architect practising in that American city who, unknown to both men at the time, would all-to-soon become the designer of the young Massey's death memorial.

∾

The Canada of the 1870s was a much different country than the Canada of today. Back then, agriculture was the pre-eminent force in the development and growth of the young nation. To supply the needs of the thousands of farmers diligently working the country's vast expanse of farm fields the little foundry in Newcastle, Ontario, was taxed far beyond its capabilities. There was only one answer to that problem and in 1879 Charles, as vice-president of the company and with the obvious concurrence of his father announced that the company would move to modern new facilities on the western outskirts of the burgeoning provincial capital, Toronto, and be renamed the Massey Manufacturing Company.

Just three years after the company moved into its new plant on the southwest corner of King Street and Strachan Avenue, a site that was north of the Toronto Industrial Exhibition (where the company had won numerous certificates and prizes for their implements) and adjacent to the tracks of both the Northern and Grand Trunk railways (each of which was extremely important to ensure quick delivery of raw materials and the rapid delivery of finished products), Massey was doing a million dollars worth of business annually, more than ten times the value of all products produced in the small Newcastle foundry in 1870, the company's inaugural year.

The future looked bright for the Canadian company whose products were soon to be tilling, harrowing and reaping fields world-wide. Then the unthinkable happened. Thirty-five-year-old Charles Massey contracted the dreaded typhoid fever and on February 12, 1884, died. Two days later, because winter burials were virtually impossible due to the frozen ground, he was interred in the vault at the recently opened Mt. Pleasant Cemetery north of the city. On May 1 Charles was buried in an area of the cemetery described as Triangle 7 where a decade later the imposing Massey catafalque would be erected to a design of famed Toronto architect Edward James Lennox. On October 6, 1894, Charles Massey's remains were moved to the newly constructed mausoleum along with those of his brother Fred Victor, who had died in April 1890, at the age of just twenty-two.

Less than two years later, Hart Massey was reunited with his sons following the patriarch's death at the age of 73.

Other Massey progeny grasped the business reigns and as the years went by the company continued its ascent eventually becoming the world's pre-eminent farm implement manufacturer. In recent years the historic Massey name vanished when the company became part of Verity Corporation.

∽

It is difficult to find words that can sufficiently characterize the magnificent success attending the opening of Massey Music Hall last evening. The splendid building with its artistic decorations and its expansive greatness was literally crowded with a throng of over 4,000 people. No event in the history of Toronto has yet occurred that was so signally and happily inaugurated as the opening of this grand structure.

...The Evening Telegram, Friday, June 15, 1894

These words were typical of the numerous accolades heaped on the city's new music hall by the local press. It certainly seemed as if Hart Massey had done the right thing when he agreed to honor his music-loving son Charley's memory by giving to the citizens of Toronto "an auditorium spacious, substantial and comfortable where public meetings, conventions, musical and other entertainments, etc., could be given, admitting of the largest number of people attending and enjoying them at a minimum cost of admission."

This in spite of comments made by a few unimpressed wags, one of whom suggested that the $152,390.75 cost of the hall would have been better spent on a poor house for the impoverished, downtrodden Massey employees. Needless to say this anonymous detractor was noticeably absent from the opening evening's complimentary ticket list.

The idea of honoring his son's memory with a modern auditorium had first entered Hart's mind following a hugely successful choral festival held just two years after Charley's untimely demise. In order to accommodate the numerous performers (1,000 choir members, a 100-piece orchestra, a children's choir and a selection of renown soloists) plus seating for the large crowds eager to attend the June 15, 16 and 17, 1886, extravaganza it was necessary for Dr. Frederick Torrington, the event's musical director, to book the multi-purpose Caledonia Rink on Mutual Street, a barn of a building that had been constructed in 1873.

Toronto did have a number of fairly large halls in 1886, but the anticipated crowds wishing to see and hear Torrington's planned festival precluded the use of more traditional facilities like the Horticultural Pavilion in Allan Gardens (erected 1878, destroyed by fire 1902), the Grand Opera House on Adelaide Street West (erected 1874, destroyed by fire 1879, rebuilt and demolished in 1927), the Princess Theatre on King Street West (built as the Academy of Music in 1889, expropriated and demolished in 1930 for the extension of University Avenue Queen to Front Street).

Torrington, who would go on to establish the now internationally famous Mendelssohn Choir in the same year the new auditorium would open, encouraged Massey to pursue his project and eventually Sidney Badgley, the young Canadian-born architect Massey had met during his time in Cleveland, was

188

engaged to design a 3,500-seat auditorium. The location of the hall was still undetermined, a fact that put severe limitations on the architect's final plans. In fact, it wasn't until 1892 that title to the parcel of land at the southwest corner of Victoria and Shuter streets was acquired. Soon the wreckers were busily tearing apart William Armitage's little grocery store, John Shand's tiny shoemaking shop and the meager frame houses of Francis Prott, Maggie Watson, Charlie Ellis and George Studd.

The dust had barely settled when, on September 20, 1893, the cornerstone of Hart Massey's new music hall was "well and truly laid" by the patriarch's six-year-old grandson Vincent. Fifty-nine years later the young-

The Hall's benefactor, Hart Almerin Massey.

ster would be recognized on his own merits when he was appointed Canada's seventeenth and first Canadian-born governor-general.

Just 237 days later, and with great ceremony, the new Massey Music Hall embarked on its first century.

SETTING SAIL

June 19, 1994

In a couple of weeks Toronto will be host to the largest-ever gathering of sail-ing ships on the Great Lakes. At press time, twenty-five majestic brigs, schooners and seaway-size "tall ships" from ports around the world are set to glide into Toronto Harbour to help celebrate the romantic age of sail and Harbourfront Centre's twentieth anniversary. The event kicks off in the early evening of Wednesday, June 29, with a sailpast from the fleet's anchorage in Humber Bay, through the West Gap and along the city's waterfront. The public is invited to view this spectacular sight from Harbourfront's seawall between York and Rees streets.

For the next few days the public is also invited to come aboard the vessels using a special pass available at seven dollars each from select Bay stores around Metro (Queen Street, Yorkdale, Scarborough, Mississauga).

As part of the six-day event there will also be concerts, arts and crafts exhibits, fireworks, food and numerous free activities for all ages. Sun readers also have the opportunity to participate in their own sail past on board the his-

Schooners moored at the foot of Brock Street, 1862.

toric sidewheeler *Trillium* which will depart from the Toronto Ferry Docks at 1:30 PM, June 30, July 1, 2 and 3. After visiting the "tall ships" *Trillium* will sail to Centre Island returning to the mainland at approximately 2:30 PM. Passenger capacity will be limited to 500 so plan to arrive early. Using the special *SUN/TRILLIUM* coupon that will appear daily in the paper the fare for the voyage will be five dollars for adults, three dollars for seniors and children (fourteen and under).

∾

The presence of sailing vessels in Toronto Harbour is, of course, nothing new. In the 1850s and '60s the Port of Toronto was frequently filled with graceful, and not-so-graceful schooners each of which was filled to capacity with either grain of lumber destined for markets on the American side of the Great Lakes. These products of the hinterland around the city would have been transported to the waterfront by other ships, railway cars or horse-drawn wagons.

In the rare, old photo taken in 1862 several large schooners waiting to load grain or timber are seen moored at the foot of Brock Street, the southerly extension to the water's edge of the modern Spadina Avenue. When ready they would be towed out of the bay by tugs such as the *Golden City*, their sails would then be spread, and off they'd head for any one of a number of American ports.

The large structure in the right background is the massive wooden grain elevator of the Northern Railway, the province's pioneer railway whose first locomotive chugged out of the city just nine years before this picture was taken. This elevator was destroyed in a huge fire that swept through the tinder dry structure in 1869. A second elevator opened on the site soon after the flames had been extinguished and it too succumbed to flames in 1908.

Faintly visible to the extreme left of the photo is one of the Northern's wood-burning locomotives moving too fast for the slow glass plate negatives of the day, thereby blurring the image.

In the foreground timber cut in the forests north of the young city awaits shipment.

One of the most famous "tall ships" to have ever visited the Port of Toronto was the majestic schooner *Bluenose*. Launched at Lunenburg, Nova Scotia, in 1921 the sleek craft was designed for both work and play; that is, to fish the Grand Banks and to race. On numerous occasions *Bluenose* captured the coveted International Fisherman's Trophy emblematic of the fastest of the fishing vessels of the north Atlantic. She also held the record for the largest catch of fish to be brought into Lunenburg Harbour. So widespread was *Bluenose's* fame that her likeness has appeared on the dime since 1937. The historic vessel was sold in 1942 to a West Indies trading company and was wrecked off Haiti four years later. A replica, *Bluenose II*, was launched in 1963 and has appeared in Toronto Harbour several times.

In the view accompanying this column we see the original *Bluenose* arriving in Toronto Harbour on May 23, 1933. She is under the command of her captain Angus Walters who not only conceived the idea of building the vessel to promote Canadian craftsmanship, but Walters also put his life savings into her creation. For many years national pride in this gracious craft and her numerous accomplishments did much to unite the country. Her betrayal in 1942 was felt strongly coast to coast.

After a stint on public view at the 1933 Century of Progress fair in Chicago followed by a three-month tour of Upper Great Lake ports, *Bluenose* returned to Toronto where she wintered remaining in the city throughout much of the following year to be part of Toronto's Centennial celebrations.

Canada's most famous schooner, *Bluenose,* enters Toronto Harbour, May 23, 1933.
(THC)

FROM THE HUNT TO THE SKIES

June 26, 1994

O n the east side of Avenue Road, a block or so north of Eglinton, is a collection of buildings, some old, some new. Over the years these buildings have served a variety of uses, most recently as an educational facility for the Canadian Armed Forces. As a result of federal government budget cuts school will be out for good this coming Thursday.

The first tenant of the Avenue Road site was the Eglinton Hunt Club, whose predecessor, the Toronto Hunt, was established in 1843 as a social and hunt club primarily for officers serving in the British Army stationed in Toronto. Initially, the club held Gymkhanas, point-to-point and racing meets at various locations in and around the city. It wasn't until 1895 that the Toronto Hunt acquired a permanent home purchasing a large tract of property on the south

Seen in this 1920 aerial view of the Eglinton Hunt Club (with outdoor track and stables) are Pears' brickyard and kilns (top left), and water tank on Roselawn Avenue (centre bottom). Narrow path crossing left to right is Avenue Road.

side of the dusty Kingston Road on the eastern outskirts of Toronto at Scarborough Heights.

In 1898, the electric street railway tracks on the Kingston Road were extended easterly from Blantyre Avenue to the Hunt Club property and before long the forested areas surrounding the club began to fill with tiny bungalows and paved streets. To satisfy those members who wished to "ride to the hounds" it was obvious that another location was necessary.

About 1909 the stables and kennels were moved to Thornhill. This was followed a decade later by the purchase of land closer to the city, a piece of property in a sparsely populated area north of the Third Concession Road (now Eglinton Avenue) not far from the sprawling brickyard and kilns of James Pears (the latter now the site of Eglinton – called Pears when I was a kid – Park). Within a few years this new site, first known as the Toronto Hunt, Eglinton Stables, then as the Eglinton Hunt Club, had stables for 150 horses, an indoor arena and outdoor show ring complete with grandstand.

In 1928–29, an enlarged riding school was added as was a new clubhouse designed in the style of an English country manor by prominent Toronto architect Vaux Chadwick. Today, Chadwick's creation remains as a gem on the former hunt club property.

In the years that followed, the Eglinton Hunt fell onto hard fiscal times. With war with Germany imminent in early 1939, the federal government stepped in and purchased the property for $55,000. It would be here, in the suburban quietness north of a bustling city, that research into various facets of

Canadian Forces Staff School on the east side of Avenue Road (view looks north from Elwood Blvd.) just before closure June 1994, showing 1928–29 clubhouse, guard house and 1950s addition.

the new science of aviation medicine could be carried out in relative obscurity under the guidance of Sir Frederick Banting, co-discoverer of insulin.

The RCAF's No. 1 Clinical Investigation Unit (CIU), as the former hunt club became known, soon became a hive of activity as scientists and technicians eagerly sought answers to the problems of high altitude flying. Using North America's first human centrifuge, installed at the Avenue Road site in 1940, Banting's associate Dr. Wilbur Franks was able to improve upon his water-filled Franks Flying Suit, a garment that helped alleviate the often deadly affects of high gravitational forces. A variant of his suit, using air in place of water, would soon give Allied pilots a distinct advantage over their airborne adversaries. Modern-day astronauts continue to rely on the so-called G-suit to protect them on dangerous missions into space.

As the need for more aircrew increased, the RCAF's No. 1 Initial Training School took over part of the Avenue Road property adding to the mix of activities on the site.

Following the end of the war administration offices and training facilities for both the Institute of Aviation Medicine (as No. 1 CIU was renamed) and RCAF auxiliary and air cadet squadrons took over the site. Then, in 1960 the air force established a staff school on the site with the first forty-six officers graduating in December of that year. Thirty-four years and 10,000 graduates later the Canadian Forces Staff School closed.

Future uses of the former hunt club/RCAF site are presently being explored by community groups and government officials

My thanks to Lt. Commander Cal Mofford and the Canadian Aviation Historical Society (Peter Allen's fascinating article on the Frank's Flying Suit appears in the Winter 1983 edition of the CAHS Journal) for assistance in preparing this article.

TORONTO'S MOST WANTED

July 3, 1994

Edwin Alonzo Boyd, now there's a name from Toronto's not so gentle past. It was like being swept back in time more than four decades when the media recently announced that the front man of the famous, or should it be infamous, Boyd Gang would shed his anonymity for a few moments in order to testify at a murder trial in Kingston.

A little background on Edwin and his associates is in order for those readers who are new to our community (or younger than forty-two years of age 'cause that's how many years its been since Boyd was despatched to the Kingston Penitentiary supposedly for life).

The notorious Boyd Gang was captured in this decrepid North York barn on September 16, 1952, following a lengthy chase up the Don Valley. Did someone recognize the importance of the location years later by calling a nearby street Chase Road?

Edwin Alonzo Boyd was born in 1914, the eldest of three boys. Ironically, as it turned out, his father was a well-respected Toronto police officer. Edwin grew up in the Danforth-Woodbine part of town and attended nearby Earl Beatty Public School.

Following his mother's death, the fifteen-year-old left school to try his luck in western Canada. With the onset of the Great Depression Boyd, like most people, found the going tough. Unlike most people, however, he decided to take the easy way out and after committing a few minor misdemeanors got serious and robbed a service station. He was quickly apprehended and spent the next two and a half years in jail.

Upon his return to Toronto, and with an eagerness displayed by thousands of young Canadians to come to the aid of Great Britain, Boyd signed up with a local militia unit and spent several months guarding the Welland Canal against hordes of perceived enemy agents. Deciding that overseas in the thick of things was what he really wanted, Boyd joined the famous Royal Regiment of Canada and was soon fighting for his life in occupied France.

Boyd escaped, returned to England, got married and applied to be reassigned to the newly established Provost Corps. Boyd liked motorcycles. He'd get to see a lot of those, especially in the post war years when they were usually operated by a burly policeman headed in his direction.

Following VE-Day, Boyd came home and obtained employment as a motorman on the old two-man Yonge streetcars frequently crewing with one or other of his brothers who were also employed by the TTC. Had Boyd remained on track, chances are he would have gone underground as an operator on Toronto's new Yonge subway.

Unfortunately, Boyd opted for another type of underground, the illicit version, and on September 9, 1949, robbed his first bank. Twenty-five months and six stick-ups later, Boyd was finally caught.

Sentenced to do time in the Don Jail, it was there that Boyd met up with a couple of particularly bad characters, Leonard and William Jackson (same surname, no relation). On November 4, 1951, the trio escaped from the ancient prison.

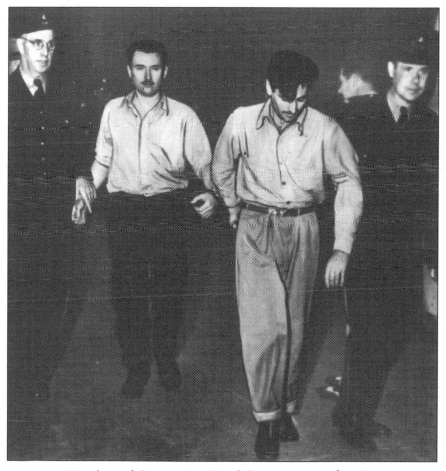

Members of the notorious Boyd Gang are captured, again.
(*Courtesy* Toronto Telegram/Toronto Sun)

Though Willie Jackson was captured just six weeks later, another unsavory individual joined what had now become known as the Boyd Gang and soon local banks were again under siege.

On March 6, 1952, the gang's bank robbing antics turned deadly when Lennie Jackson and the newcomer, Steve Suchan, were involved in the shooting of Sergeant of Detectives Edmund Tong. The Toronto policeman died seventeen days later.

Did the sign describe the end of the chase?

In the greatest manhunt the city had ever witnessed the gang members were again rounded up, Lennie Jackson following a shoot-out in Montreal, during which Suchan was also captured, and Boyd during a raid on his Heath Street West residence. Pending trial the four were reunited in the old Don Jail where, on September 8, 1952, the unbelievable happened. Once again the quartet escaped.

For the next eight days the world appeared to come to a complete standstill as everyone searched for the Boyd Gang. Finally, on September 16 they were captured while cowering in a deserted barn just west of Leslie Street in the bushland north of the city.

This time gang members would stand trial. Willie Jackson was to spend fourteen years in the Kingston Pen. He was paroled and moved to Vancouver where he may still live in anonymity.

Edwin Alonzo Boyd was given life, paroled in 1962, broke parole, jailed again and paroled for a second time in 1966. He too moved west to live in anonymity, returning to Kingston a few weeks ago to testify in a murder trial. Police-killers Steve Suchan and Leonard Jackson were hanged at the Don Jail on December 12, 1956.

Ꮽ

So far everything you've read is based on fact. Now for some "Boyd Gang trivia" based on a theory I developed while researching a future book that will deal with the origins of Metro street names. Just to the southwest of the busy Leslie-Sheppard intersection in North York is a small thoroughfare called Chase Road. Cross-referencing its modern-day location with aerial photos and line maps accompanying newspaper coverage of the Boyd Gang's capture nearly forty-two years ago, it appears that Chase Road was laid out in close proximity to that old barn where the gang hid out. Was its name selected to mark the end of the chase through the Don valley? I wonder.

A CAPITAL IDEA

July 10, 1994

One of the photos commissioned for the 1857 report promoting Toronto as the capital of the Province of Canada is this view looking north on York Street from King. Note Osgoode Hall on Queen Street in the distance. This is one of the oldest photos of Toronto in existence.
(CTA)

Another Canada Day has come and gone. That makes a total of 127 of them (though I remember when they were called Dominion Days) since four of Great Britain's North American colonies confederated under terms outlined in the British North America Act thereby creating the original Dominion of Canada. Members of that 1867 version of our country were the Province of Canada (the union of Canada East and Canada West – today's Quebec and Ontario, respectively – proclaimed in 1841) plus the provinces of New Brunswick and Nova Scotia. Other jurisdictions joined the family over the ensuing years (Manitoba in 1870, British Columbia in 1871, Prince Edward Island in 1873, Alberta and Saskatchewan in 1905 and Newfoundland in 1949).

Certainly the most visible event that takes place each July 1 are the festivities on Parliament Hill in the nation's capital. But had Queen Victoria not listened to her advisors and paid more attention to a document forwarded to her by John Hutchison those

Same view, 1994. Osgoode Hall, though still there, is hardly visible in amongst York Street's skyscrapers.

festivities might have been held right here in Toronto.

The year was 1857. Government officials of the Province of Canada (as mentioned, today's Ontario and Quebec) were desperately trying to come up with a permanent location for the provincial capital city. In the sixteen years that had passed since the Province of Canada's creation in 1841 that honour had been held by Quebec City, Toronto (both were the site of the capital on two separate occasions), Kingston and Montreal.

This practice was unacceptable for a number of reasons, not the least of which was the cost of relocating the huge numbers of bureaucrats every few years. In an attempt to solve the problem the elected members were asked to select a city. Unfortunately a consensus could not be reached (what was determined, however, was that Ottawa was a consistent last choice) and so it was decided to ask an unbiased arbitrator to decide the issue. And who better to approach than the British Monarch? It would be up to Queen Victoria to select the site of the capital of the Province of Canada.

To assist with her (or is it Her) decision, officials of each community seeking capital city status were requested to contribute memorials for her perusal. In total, six cities entered the race; Toronto, Quebec, Montreal, Kingston, Ottawa and, as a late starter, Hamilton.

Toronto's submission, dated March 28, 1857, and signed by one-term mayor John Hutchison, touched on matters related to the city's increasing business and commercial activity, its proximity to large centers of population, defensibility and the fact that Toronto was served by no less than four railway lines.

To make the submission special, officials decided to take advantage of the latest technological wonder of the day and include a selection of black and white photographs of their city. These views are some of the oldest views of Toronto in existence.

In spite of Toronto's valiant attempt, the Queen chose Ottawa as the site of the capital of the Province of Canada. Her selection made public during the Speech from the Throne on January 10, 1859. But both Toronto and Quebec had turns as capital before Ottawa became the permanent site in October of 1865. With the creation of Canada on July 1, 1867, Ottawa became the capital of the new dominion.

RAIL KING'S MANSION

July 17, 1994

Sir William Mackenzie, 1849–1923.

For the past couple of years my wife and I have spent our holidays wandering the backroads of Great Britain in a rented car, exploring that country's ancient towns and villages and staying each evening in a different bed and breakfast establishment many steeped in history.

Recently, while wandering the backroads right here in Ontario, we came across a remarkable bed and breakfast establishment right on Metro's doorstep that too is steeped in history. And they take Canadian money at par.

On the north side of Highway 48 in the little village of Kirkfield is the Sir William Mackenzie Inn, a forty-room mansion erected in 1888 by the man that was to become known internationally as "the railway king of Canada". Following Sir William's death on December 5, 1923 the gracious residence was converted into a boarding school for young women only to be abandoned many years later and left to face an uncertain future.

The years went by and while several attempts were made to breathe new life into the old place nothing clicked. Nothing, that is, until Paul and Joan Scott discovered the forsaken structure a couple of years ago. Then on June 15, 1993, after hundreds of hours of tender loving care plus many thousands of dollars in restoration capital, the historic structure reopened as a charming six-room inn.

Billy Mackenzie was born in a small log cabin on his father's farm near Kirkfield on October 30, 1849. As a young man, Mackenzie took to teaching the children of Eldon Township, but it wasn't long before the country school-master tired of the daily "3 Rs" routine. Canada was young and eager and so was Mackenzie.

It was obvious that there was a lot more money to be made exploiting the acres and acres of dense forest that surrounded Kirkfield and soon Mackenzie found himself in the lumber business with his brother Alex. The pair built numerous wooden structures in and around their hometown several of which still stand. But the real money was to be found in building the stations, bridges and roadbeds for those new-fangled railways that were rapidly laying rails all over the countryside.

Mackenzie's chance came in 1874 when the firm run by the Mackenzie boys was selected to construct several bridges and buildings for the newly chartered Victoria Railway that was to run between the nearby community of Lindsay and the Ottawa River. Their work was completed on time and on budget. It was obvious that Billy Mackenzie liked his new role as a railway builder.

He worked on countless other projects, but it wasn't until 1884 when he bid on and won the contract to build a section of the new Canadian Pacific Railway through the Rockies that his skills were truly tested. It was a difficult assignment. Nevertheless, once again he was equal to the task.

The magnificent Sir William Mackenzie Inn.

It was on this project that Mackenzie first met up with Donald Mann (whose future residence, Fallingbrook, would eventually lend its name to a nearby street). Together they would construct the country's second transcontinental railroad, the Canadian Northern Railway. It was to become Mackenzie's greatest disappointment when, less than five years after the line's opening in 1915, the CNR became just a segment of the new Canadian National Railways, the federal government's potpourri of five financially troubled rail enterprises each of which had steamed into business with such grandiose plans.

But that disappointment was still decades in the future. In the 1880s Mackenzie was rich. So rich, in fact, that in 1888 he returned to his hometown of Kirkfield and built for his growing family a fabulous $18,000, three-storey mansion, the grandest thing the villagers had ever seen. More than a century later the Mackenzie residence would be reborn as the Sir William Mackenzie Inn.

Mackenzie still had much to do. In 1891, he purchased the rights to operate what had been since 1861 Toronto's horse-powered street railway system. The magic of that newest wonder of the age, electricity, fascinated both Mackenzie and Toronto city council. Accordingly, work on converting the new Toronto Railway Company to this innovative form of motive power was undertaken almost immediately and completed by the end of 1894.

With more and more of his time being spent in Toronto, Mackenzie's wife Margaret arranged for the purchase of the baronial residence of real estate developer S.H. Janes on the Avenue Road hill. It was here at *Benvenuto* that Sir William (he had been knighted in 1911) died on December 5, 1923.

The full and fascinating life of Sir William Mackenzie has been captured in Rae Fleming's book "The Railway King of Canada" (UBC Press, Vancouver, 1991) which I recommend to anyone interested in Canadian history.

Further information on the William Mackenzie Inn can be obtained from the Scotts, c/o P.O. Box 255B, Kirkfield, Ontario K0M 2B0.

TOUGH LOAD TO MOVE

July 24, 1994

"Many city streetcars in downtown Toronto were held up for considerable periods of time today as a local moving company blocked tracks while transferring a colossal cargo from the CPR yard on Wellington Street to the corner of Yonge and Melinda streets. The tie-up nearly resulted in the streetcar company inspectors and Mr. Colville, owner and general superintendent of the moving company coming to blows."

On July 21, 1914 a strange procession made its way east along Adelaide Street (all the buildings in the view were demolished for the University Avenue extension in 1929–30) as a *Harbord* streetcar brings up the rear. *(T-D Archives)*

No, this isn't a traffic report flashed to us from Daryl Dahlmer or Henry Shannon flying high over the modern city of Toronto, but rather it's part of a newspaper account describing an incident that took place in the heart of our city exactly eighty years ago last Thursday.

The object being moved through the streets that hot July 21, 1914, was a massive forty-ton steel door frame measuring 12' x 15' x 3' destined for the new Dominion Bank Building under construction at the southwest corner of Yonge and King streets. When fitted with its thirty-ton, seven and a half-foot diameter door (that was scheduled to arrive the following week) the imposing combination would guard entry to the country's largest bank vault.

And the motive power used to propel this giant cargo from the Canadian Pacific railway freight yard (located just south of the King and Simcoe streets intersection where Roy Thomson Hall is situated today) to the bank site, eighteen huge horses each of which strained and sweated profusely in the summer heat responding as best they could to the yells and whistles of William Colville's burly nineteen-member moving crew.

Because of the poor condition of Wellington Street east of Simcoe, the route selected by the movers to get from the rail yard to the south end of the new bank building at King and Yonge meant that the strange procession would first go west on Wellington, then north on Peter, back east along Adelaide, turn south on Bay, continue east on Wellington and finally north on Yonge to the Melinda Street corner where a huge hole in the structure under construction had been left through which the frame (and later the massive vault door) would pass.

Apparently the moving company had neglected to advise officials of the street railway that the cargo would travel along Adelaide Street. As a result several streetcars on the Harbord route were caught in the procession causing a delay of nearly thirty minutes. The inspectors were not amused and were it not for the timely intervention of several large police officers there's little doubt that a donnybrook would have erupted.

The Toronto-born Dominion Bank first opened for business in the old Harris Building at 40 King Street East in 1871. Eight years later the bank moved into a newly constructed five-storey building along the street at the south west corner of Yonge. The years went by and the bank prospered. Soon officials felt that a new head office building was necessary and the local architectural firm of Darling and Pearson were engaged to design a new structure to replace the old one on the Yonge and King site. Excavation work on the impressive structure commenced on May 29, 1913, with the first tenants moving in just 13thirteen months later. The banking facilities, including a bank vault with the door frame that held up city traffic that hot day 80 years ago, were ready in mid-October, 1914.

The vault's destination was the new Dominion Bank Building (now the Toronto-Dominion Bank Building) at Yonge and King streets.

In 1955, the Dominion Bank and Bank of Toronto joined forces creating the Toronto-Dominion Bank. Though the bank's head office is now in the T-D Centre, the 1913–14 Dominion Bank has been nicely restored and still stands proudly at the King and Yonge corner.

THE OLD MILL TURNING EIGHTY

July 31, 1994

This coming Thursday marks the eightieth birthday of one of Metro's true landmarks, the Old Mill. Now, before I get into difficulties with other history buffs, the Old Mill to which I'm referring is the one that started out on August 4, 1914, as the Old Mill Tearoom. To be sure there is another "old mill," the one that stands just to the east of today's tea room/restaurant/ convention and meeting room complex.

The "old mill" of William Gamble after which today's Old Mill Restaurant is named. Some cattle ambling across the Humber add to the charm of this turn-of-the-century penny postcard.

OLD MILL #1

Though now simply a rather forlorn ruin, the original "old mill" had been erected for pioneer settler William Gamble in 1848. Twice flames visited the mill, the second conflagration being the most serious. It erupted one cold winter's day in late 1881 when a pipe leading from an overheated stove, glowing red hot from attempts to keep dozens of baskets of apples stored on the upper floors from freezing, broke resulting in the wooden floors being set alight. The remoteness of the site resulted in the mill being totally gutted. Never rebuilt, the original "old mill" minus its roof and windows stood neglected, eventually becoming just an interesting old ruin, the subject of poems and penny postcards.

The Gamble Mill was just one of many pioneer mills erected adjacent to the Humber River specifically to take advantage of the river's fast flowing waters to turn the numerous milling and grinding wheels. In recent years flood control dams (constructed as a result of the devastation wrought by Hurricane Hazel forty years ago) and straightening of the watercourse have resulted in a markedly decreased flow of water.

Perhaps the most important of these early mills was the King's Saw Mill situated a short distance downstream from the Gamble Mill and erected in the fall of 1793 (the same year Toronto was established) under orders issued by none other than Lieutenant-Governor Simcoe himself. The King's Mill is regarded by many as Metropolitan Toronto's first industry. Timber cut from the banks of the Humber and shaped and sized in the King's Mill was used in the construction of many of our community's first structures.

OLD MILL #2

It would have been tough for Robert Home Smith to get any press coverage in the local papers when he opened his brand new Old Mill Tearoom that warm summer day eighty years ago. Seems the papers were preoccupied covering a slightly more important event. On the very day Smith unlocked the Old Mill's doors for the first time, Great Britain decided to declare war on Germany. The First World War, the war that was supposed to end before Christmas, was underway. Of course, Home Smith was concerned, but life goes on.

Smith was an amazing fellow. His many achievements prior to his untimely death in 1935 are far to numerous to review in just one column.

Born in Stratford, Ontario, July 12, 1877, Smith studied law at Toronto's Osgoode Hall. Because profound deafness prevented him from embarking on a practice of his own (such challenges were much more incapacitating back then) he decided to join the National Trust Company as Manager of the Estates Department.

His interest in land dealings grew rapidly and before long he personally owned thousands of acres in Peel County, Niagara-on-the-Lake, Caledon Township and, before he was thirty years of age, some 3,000 acres of prime property stretched out alongside the banks of the beautiful Humber River.

In 1912, Smith offered the public a chance to purchase sites in his "Humber Valley Survey," a development that included five subdivisions; Riverside, Bridge End, Bâby Point, The Old Mill and The Glebe. To ensure his clients' recreational and social needs were well provided for Smith built the Old Mill Tearoom two years later. Over the ensuing years, this Old Mill has grown dramatically and while it now hosts business meetings, international conferences, wedding receptions (the Old Mill even has its own chapel on site) many guests prefer to simply be part of a long-time Toronto tradition as they dine and dance the evening away at the Old Mill.

PRINTED IN CANADA